Italy

Italy

BY JEAN F. BLASHFIELD

Enchantment of the World™
Second Series

Children's Press®

An Imprint of Scholastic Inc.

New York Toronto London Auckland Sydney
Mexico City New Delhi Hong Kong
Danbury, Connecticut

Frontispiece: Historical boats ply the Grand Canal in Venice.

Consultant: Dennis Looney, Chair, Department of French and Italian, University of Pittsburgh

Please note: All statistics are as up-to-date as possible at the time of publication.

Book production by Herman Adler

Library of Congress Cataloging-in-Publication Data

Blashfield, Jean F.
 Italy / by Jean F. Blashfield.
     p. cm.—(Enchantment of the world. Second series)
 Includes bibliographical references and index.
 ISBN-13: 978-0-531-12099-6
 ISBN-10: 0-531-12099-6
 1. Italy—Juvenile literature. I. Title.
DG417.B58 2008
945—dc22   2007052381

Italy

Contents

Cover photo:
The Leaning
Tower of Pisa

CHAPTER

 ONE Experiencing Italy 8

 TWO Land and Sea 14

THREE The Natural World 28

FOUR Through the Ages 40

FIVE Governing the Republic 64

SIX Italy at Work 76

SEVEN The Italian People 86

 EIGHT Religion in Italian Life 94

NINE Creativity and Skill 104

TEN The Best of Life 116

Sardinia

Timeline.....................**128**

Fast Facts....................**130**

To Find Out More...........**134**

Index **136**

Gondolier

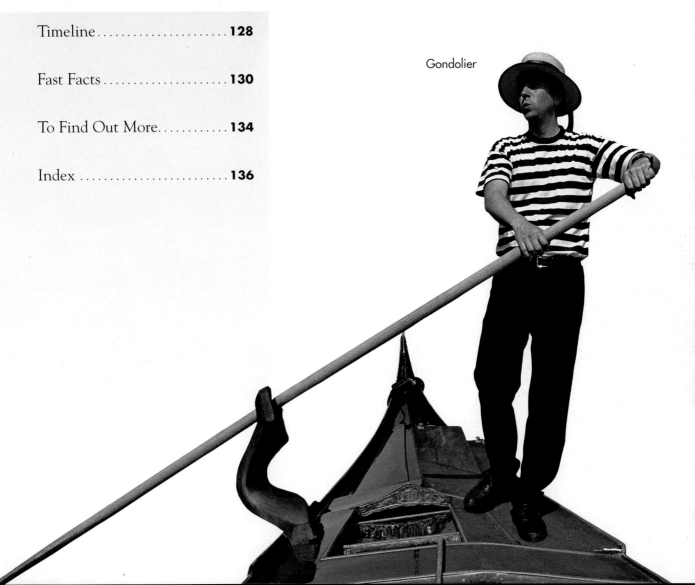

Experiencing
Italy

Y
OU'RE STANDING IN A SQUARE IN A MEDIEVAL TOWN, staring awestruck at the many flags and banners that decorate the surrounding buildings. Suddenly, the sound of hooves echoes around you. Young jockeys, riding horses bareback, race around the square, or piazza, three times. The prize is a silk flag, the *Palio*. This is part of an eight-hundred-year-old festival that is held twice each summer in the town of Siena.

Opposite: **The Piazza del Campo in Siena is one of Italy's grandest medieval squares.**

Riders race around Siena's Piazza del Campo during the Palio race in 2005.

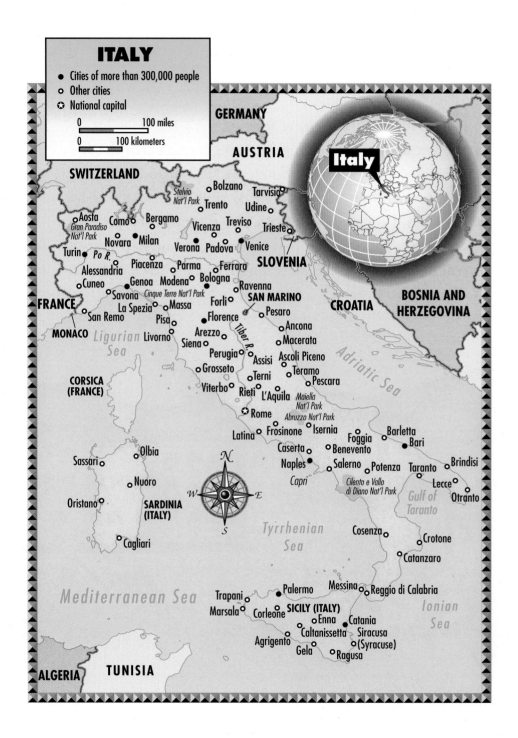

ITALY

- Cities of more than 300,000 people
- Other cities
- National capital

0   100 miles

0   100 kilometers

Italy

GERMANY

AUSTRIA

SWITZERLAND

SLOVENIA

Stelvio Nat'l Park

Bolzano

Tarvisio

Trento

Udine

Aosta

Como

Bergamo

Treviso

Trieste

Gran Paradiso Nat'l Park

Vicenza

Novara

Milan

Verona

Padova

Venice

Turin

Po R.

Alessandria

Piacenza

Parma

Ferrara

SLOVENIA

Cuneo

Genoa

Modena

Bologna

Ravenna

Savona

Cinque Terre Nat'l Park

Forli

SAN MARINO

CROATIA

BOSNIA AND HERZEGOVINA

FRANCE

La Spezia

Massa

Florence

Pesaro

MONACO

San Remo

Pisa

Arezzo

Ancona

Adriatic Sea

Livorno

Siena

Macerata

Ligurian Sea

Perugia

Assisi

Ascoli Piceno

CORSICA (FRANCE)

Grosseto

Terni

Teramo

Viterbo

Rieti

Pescara

L'Aquila

Maiella Nat'l Park

Rome

Abruzzo Nat'l Park

Latina

Frosinone

Isernia

Barletta

Foggia

Bari

Olbia

Caserta

Benevento

Sassari

Naples

Salerno

Potenza

Taranto

Brindisi

Nuoro

Capri

Lecce

Cilento e Vallo di Diano Nat'l Park

Gulf of Taranto

Otranto

Oristano

SARDINIA (ITALY)

Cosenza

Crotone

Cagliari

Tyrrhenian Sea

Catanzaro

Mediterranean Sea

Trapani

Palermo

Messina

Reggio di Calabria

Marsala

Corleone

SICILY (ITALY)

Enna

Catania

Ionian Sea

Agrigento

Caltanissetta

Siracusa

Gela

Ragusa

(Syracuse)

ALGERIA

TUNISIA

N

W

E

S

Italian designer Anna Molinari presents her designs at Fashion Week in Milan.

You've saved your money and bought a ticket to Fashion Week in Milan. All the world's great clothing designers will be showing their startling and beautiful designs. You'll be one of the first to see them!

Or picture yourself in Rome. You're at a performance of the opera *Aïda*, written by Italian composer Giuseppe Verdi. You're seated amid eighteen-hundred-year-old ruins under a starry sky, listening to magnificent music.

You've got your snowboard and warm clothing so you can glide down the slopes the world's greatest skiers took during

The ruins of a Greek temple stand in Agrigento, Sicily. It was built in the fifth century B.C.

the 2006 Winter Olympics near Turin. Or perhaps it's summer, and you're going to explore the sea caves of Capri, off the coast of Naples. Later, you can take a look at the towering columns at Agrigento, among the temples the ancient Greeks built on the island of Sicily long before Italy existed.

In any one of these places, you might be one of the millions of tourists who visit Italy every year. But alongside the tourists are Italians, also appreciative of the wonders of their own country.

Italy is in southern Europe, on the northern side of the Mediterranean Sea. Within its borders are a glorious array of landscapes. In the north tower mountains tipped with glaciers. The south basks in year-round sunshine. Between are craggy cliffs, ancient farmland, rolling vineyards, and coasts with warm beaches.

The art and history of Italy are vital to European culture—indeed, to the culture of the whole world. Italy is packed full of monuments, temples, palaces, museums, and churches, many featuring astounding artwork.

But Italy is not a museum. It is a modern, vibrant nation filled with people making the most of all their country has to offer.

Scooters are a popular way to get around Italy's streets.

CHAPTER
TWO

Land and Sea

14

The small town of Altagnana sits in a valley in Tuscany.

ITALY IS SHAPED LIKE A BOOT THAT STRIDES ACROSS THE northern Mediterranean Sea. The nation includes two large islands: Sicily, near the "toe" of the boot, and Sardinia, farther to the northwest. Italy's only bordering countries are in the north: France, Switzerland, Austria, and Slovenia.

The rest of Italy borders water. The Mediterranean stretches around three sides of Italy, though in some places it has different names. The area bounded by Sicily, Sardinia, and the western shore of the boot is called the Tyrrhenian Sea. North of that is the Ligurian Sea. The Gulf of Taranto forms the arch, or instep, of the boot, while below that is the Ionian Sea. And the Adriatic Sea lies along Italy's northeastern coast.

Opposite: **The Liguria region lies along the coast near the French border.**

Italy's Geographic Features

Area: 116,313 square miles (301,249 sq km)

Highest Elevation: Monte Bianco (Mont Blanc), 15,771 feet (4,807 m)

Lowest Elevation: Sea level, along Italy's coasts

Longest River: Po River, 405 miles (652 km) long

Largest Lake: Lake Garda, 143 square miles (370 sq km)

Largest Island: Sicily, 9,925 square miles (25,706 sq km)

Coastline: About 4,700 miles (7,600 km), including all the islands

Highest Active Volcano: Mount Etna, 11,053 feet (3,369 m)

Greatest Distance North to South: 760 miles (1,220 km)

Greatest Distance East to West: 320 miles (515 km)

Average High Temperatures: January: 52°F (11°C) in Rome, 41°F (5°C) in Milan; July: 86°F (30°C) in Rome, 84°F (29°C) in Milan

Mountainous Land

Italy's boot shape comes from two ranges of mountains that together form a T. The mountains known as the Alps make the crossbar of the T as they stretch from France to Slovenia. The Apennines twist along the length of the boot from north to south.

The Alps rise at Genoa, along a part of the Ligurian shoreline known as the Italian Riviera, and stretch across northern Italy. The highest peak in Italy—and in all of Europe—is Monte Bianco (or Mont Blanc), at 15,771 feet (4,807 meters). The Dolomites, a section of the eastern Alps, have many peaks above 10,000 feet (3,000 m).

Amid the Alps lies the Italian Lake District. Lake Garda, Italy's largest lake at 143 square miles (370 square kilometers), and Lakes Como and Maggiore attract tourists to this area.

A fourteenth-century castle in Malcesine sits along the shore of Lake Garda.

Corno Grande, the highest peak in the Apennines, is just 20 miles (32 km) from the coast of the Adriatic Sea.

The Apennine Mountains are lower than the Alps and are home to only one small glacier. The highest peak in the Apennines is Corno Grande (Big Horn), at 9,560 feet (2,914 m), in the Abruzzi region of central Italy. The Apennines range from 25 miles (40 km) wide to 125 miles (200 km) wide.

Valley and Shore

Italy's only large area of flatland stretches west from the Adriatic Sea between the Alps and the northern Apennines. The region, the valley of the Po River, is called the North Italian Plain. An area called the Piedmont slopes from the plain up to the mountains.

Tunnels Through the Mountains

Traffic moves slowly on the twisting roads through the Alps. To speed things up, several tunnels have been drilled straight through the mountains. The Mont Blanc Tunnel carries road traffic between France and Italy. Opened in 1965, the tunnel is 7.3 miles (11.7 km) long.

In the 1880s, a dramatically twisting railroad tunnel was built through Saint Gotthard Pass, which also connects Italy and France. In 1980, the world's longest highway tunnel was built through the pass. It is 10.1 miles (16.3 km) long.

The Lötschberg Base Tunnel, which opened in 2007, provides a 22-mile (35 km) railway link between Switzerland and Italy. The tunnel cuts travel time through the mountains in half. It is the world's longest land tunnel.

A flat, narrow coastal plain also runs along both sides of the Apennines. Sand covers the coastal plain in many places, making beautiful, attractive beaches. In the north, the area called the Italian Riviera extends from France to La Spezia.

In some parts of southern Italy, the mountains tumble directly down to the sea, leaving little room for anything but narrow beaches and boat docks. One place like this is Amalfi, on the Sorrento Peninsula, which juts into the Tyrrhenian Sea south of Naples. The dizzying Amalfi Drive winds around cliffs that tower above the sea.

A Nation Tucked in the Mountains

The slopes of an Apennine mountain in eastern Italy hide the tiny, independent nation of San Marino. Covering only 23.5 square miles (61 sq km), it is the world's fourth-smallest nation. Only Monaco (on the French Mediterranean coast), Nauru (an island republic in the South Pacific), and Vatican City (in Rome) are smaller.

A stonecutter named Marinus led Christians fleeing persecution in Rome to this isolated spot in the year 301. He was later declared a saint, giving the nation its name. The citizens of San Marino are called Sammarinesi.

No one bothered the Christians in their mountain fortress, and they gradually developed their own society, which is now the world's oldest republic. The nation has fewer than thirty thousand citizens. They elect a council of sixty people who run the country. San Marino functions under a constitution written in 1600—the oldest written constitution that people still follow.

City in the Sea

A group of 118 tiny islands rises from a shallow lagoon on the northeast coast of the Adriatic. These islands make up the city of Venice.

People have lived on these islands for more than 1,500 years. Over the centuries, they built supports for houses on the low-lying islands by driving tree trunks into the muddy seabed. In time, Venice became an independent republic and a flourishing center of trade. By the 1300s, it had a major seafaring culture and was the most prosperous city in Europe. Today, ancient mansions and magnificent churches fill the city, reminders of its former wealth and power.

Venice remains closely tied to the sea. In some ways, this has endangered the city, because it floods frequently. The flooding has many causes. Channels that people dug so ships could reach ports changed the depth of the lagoon. For many years, the pumping of groundwater from beneath the city allowed the land to sink. Sea levels have also risen.

In 2003, workers began constructing a series of large metal plates on the seabed where the ocean enters the lagoon. When forecasters predict a very high sea, or tide, these plates will be raised, protecting the city from flooding. The project is due to be completed by 2012.

The Cinque Terre

Five ancient villages called the Cinque Terre ("Five Lands") cling to the cliffs above the Italian Riviera near La Spezia. For hundreds of years, their completely inaccessible location kept residents safe from invaders. People could reach the towns only by sea or by a treacherous footpath. Today, a railroad and a road bring many tourists to the spectacular site.

The Islands

The toe of Italy's boot aims straight at the island of Sicily, which lies across the Strait of Messina from the mainland. With an area of 9,925 square miles (25,706 sq km), it is the largest island in the Mediterranean Sea. More than five million people call this mountainous island home. Palermo, its largest city, is located on the northern coast of the island. Cave paintings found near Palermo show that humans may have occupied the area ten thousand years ago. The highest peak on Sicily is Mount Etna, an active volcano. Etna rises to about 11,053 feet (3,369 m), but its height continually changes as lava solidifies or crumbles at the top.

Nuraghi ruins on Sardinia. Nuraghi may have been used to defend the island from invaders.

Mount Etna has erupted on and off for more than two million years, but people continue to live in villages and grow crops on its fertile lower slopes.

Sardinia is slightly smaller than Sicily, at 9,301 square miles (24,089 sq km). Its smaller population makes it much less crowded than Sicily. About 3,500 years ago, a little-known group of people called the Nuraghi built many stone towers and cones (which are also called *nuraghi*) that still dot Sardinia's rugged landscape today.

As in much of Italy, mountains seem to rise directly from Sardinia's shores. The island's highest point is Mount La Marmora, at 6,017 feet (1,834 m). The island has considerably more flatland than Sicily does. This makes Sardinia more productive agriculturally, although maquis, a low-growing, scrubby plant, covers the open grassland on much of the flat part of Sardinia.

Sardinia produces most of Italy's lead and zinc as well as bauxite, feldspar, and clay. It also has coal mines along the southwestern coast.

The island of Capri lies off the end of the Sorrento Peninsula. Many sea caves break its coastline. Perhaps the most famous of these, the Blue Grotto, got its name from the way the sunlight strikes the water, making it a vivid blue.

Rumbling Mountains

Four active volcanoes shake the southern Apennines. One of these, Mount Vesuvius, lies on the shore of the Bay of Naples. The people who lived near it two thousand years ago didn't

The last eruption of Mount Vesuvius was in 1944. The eruption, shown here, lasted five days and destroyed two villages.

know it was a volcano. Then, in A.D. 79, Vesuvius suddenly blew its top and hot ash filled the sky, burying the city of Pompeii and neighboring towns. Over the centuries, Vesuvius has erupted again from time to time, often with little warning.

Mount Etna, on the island of Sicily, is more than three times higher than Vesuvius. It is one of the world's most active volcanoes, producing frequent lava flows. Italy's other two active volcanoes, Stromboli and Vulcano, belong to a group of islands called the Aeolians, off the northern coast of Sicily.

Buried Cities

During the Roman Empire, wealthy Romans took vacations in the cities of Pompeii and Herculaneum. The people in these towns did not know that nearby Mount Vesuvius doomed them. On August 24 in the year A.D. 79, the top blew off the mountain. Hot rock and ash buried Pompeii and Herculaneum. An estimated five thousand people died when their houses collapsed or they choked to death on the ash.

After the Roman Empire ended, the people in neighboring cities forgot Pompeii and Herculaneum. In the sixteenth century, an architect named Domenico Fontana found evidence that cities were buried under 20 feet (6 m) of earth. It was another two hundred years before anyone began digging.

In the 1800s, archaeologists were stunned to discover the perfectly preserved forms of people who had died trying to flee the volcano. They also uncovered graceful courtyards (right) and beautiful homes with elegant tile floors and statues. These discoveries helped scientists learn what the daily life of the ancient Romans

might have been like. In 2002, they found that the port area along the Gulf of Naples had houses built on stilts. Still more mysteries wait to be uncovered.

Earthquake at Assisi

In 1997, an earthquake in Assisi damaged frescoes by Giotto and Cimabue, two of Italy's greatest painters, in the Basilica of Saint Francis of Assisi. Fresco paintings, which are done on wet plaster walls, become part of the walls as the plaster dries.

Experts hurried to Assisi to evaluate the damage. Even as they were studying the cracked walls, more quakes sent bits of the priceless frescoes tumbling onto the experts' heads. Before the church reopened in 1999, workers put wires into the walls to prevent them from collapsing in another earthquake.

Earthquakes also strike Italy. In 1693, an estimated one hundred thousand people died in an earthquake in Sicily. The most deadly recent quake in Italy occurred near Naples in 1980. It killed three thousand people.

Climate

Italy's climate varies greatly from north to south. In the Alps, at the top of the boot, snow lingers on the highest peaks throughout the summer.

The foot of the boot has hot, dry summers and mild winters. In summer, the temperature can easily reach 90 degrees

Sicily has a dry climate
with mild winters and hot,
dry summers.

Fahrenheit (32 degrees Celsius) or higher. This climate draws many northerners to the Mediterranean beaches in the winter.

Rome, Italy's capital, is in the middle of the boot. Its average high temperature in January is about 52°F (11°C), and its average high temperature in July is 86°F (30°C). In 2003, Italy suffered a heat wave in which the temperature reached 100°F (38°C) or more throughout the summer. An estimated three thousand people, mostly elderly, died.

Rain is the heaviest during the fall and winter months. The rainiest areas are in the north. The city of Udine, in the northeast, receives about 60 inches (150 centimeters) of rain a year, but only about 18 inches (46 cm) fall on southern Sicily each year.

Looking at Italian Cities

Milan, Italy's second-largest city, is in the northwest. The city was founded in about 600 B.C. Today, it is Italy's industrial and commercial capital. Leading industries include banking, fashion, textiles, steel, and chemicals. Many visitors to Milan want to see Leonardo da Vinci's *The Last Supper*, which is painted on a wall in the Santa Maria delle Grazie monastery. Others flock to La Scala, a world-famous opera house, or visit Europe's third-largest cathedral, the Duomo (right).

Naples (below), Italy's third-largest city, is a major port on the country's southwest coast. Greeks founded Naples in about 600 B.C., and over the years, its rulers included Romans, Byzantines, Saracens, Normans, Spanish, and French. Finally, in 1861, Naples became part of the Kingdom of Italy. Today, Naples is southern Italy's center of industry, business, and culture. The

industries include textiles, steel, aircraft parts, shipbuilding, and oil refining. Narrow old streets thread through the city past churches, palaces, and museums. The Porta Capuana (a huge, sculptured gateway), the National Museum of Archaeology, and the Palazzo Reale ("Royal Palace") are a few highlights.

Turin, Italy's fourth-largest city, is located in northwest Italy at the foot of the Alps. Founded by the Taurini tribe long before the Romans ruled Italy, Turin served as the first capital of the Kingdom of Italy from 1861 to 1865. Today, it is the center of Italy's automobile industry and headquarters of the Fiat car company. People also know Turin for its leather goods, fashion design, chocolate, and winemaking. In 2006, Turin hosted the Winter Olympics.

The Natural World

ITALY HAS A WIDE VARIETY OF LANDSCAPES, RANGING FROM frigid mountain peaks to sun-drenched coasts. Because of this variation, Italy is home to many different types of plants.

Opposite: **Rocky peaks tower over colorful meadows in Puez-Geisler Nature Park in northern Italy.**

Plant Life

Long ago, forests covered large swaths of Italy. Over the centuries, people cut down trees to make room for farmland or buildings or to use as timber or fuel. Trees help prevent soil erosion on mountain slopes. Without the roots of trees to hold

Trees such as cypress and umbrella pines are planted around fields to block the wind.

the soil in place, it sometimes washes away. This is particularly important during heavy rains, when mudslides sometimes occur on barren mountain slopes. In 1998, mudslides near Sarno, south of Naples, killed several hundred people.

Italy began major replanting efforts in the 1980s, and the amount of forested land in the nation has been increasing in recent years. Today, about one-third of Italy is covered in forest. Hardy, sun-loving trees grow in the lowlands of southern Italy. These include olive, lemon, pomegranate, fig, date, and almond trees.

Truffle Sniffers

The Piedmont region is home to truffles. These relatives of mushrooms are highly prized. The truffles grow underground, among the roots of such trees as oaks, hazels, and beeches. When they are ripe, they give off an odor that well-trained dogs can sniff out. (In France, truffle hunters often use pigs instead of dogs.)

Truffles are so highly valued by chefs that they draw high prices. In 2007, a dog named Rocco discovered a truffle in Tuscany, a region in central Italy, that weighed 3.3 pounds (1.5 kilograms). It sold at auction for US$330,000, a world record for a truffle.

Chestnut, cypress, and oak trees grow on the lower slopes of the mountains. Beech trees are also common. Higher up are forests of pine and fir. Alpine, or high-mountain, plants generally grow low to the ground. This makes them better able to withstand the hard, cold winds that blow in the high mountains. Grass-covered valleys dot the mountains. Herds of sheep, cattle, and goats often graze in these areas.

A weathered oak tree grows on an Italian hillside.

Animal Life

As Italy has become more and more populated over the centuries, many of the big animals that once roamed the peninsula have disappeared. Today, about ninety different mammal species live in Italy. Fourteen of them are endangered. Brown bears were once common in the mountains of Italy, but today only a few remain. Likewise, wolves once lived in the mountains across Italy, but their numbers declined dramatically in the late nineteenth and early twentieth centuries.

Recent efforts by conservationists have resulted in an increase in the brown bear population in Italy.

A Symbol of Italy

The Italian wolf is Italy's unofficial national animal. The wolf plays a large role in the legend of the founding of Rome.

The story goes that a princess named Rhea Silvia bore twins named Romulus and Remus. Their father was the god Mars. The princess's jealous brother ordered the boys killed, but friends of their mother set them afloat in a basket on the Tiber River. The basket caught on the roots of a fig tree. A female wolf found them there and nursed the infant boys. A shepherd who discovered the boys raised them as his own.

When the boys grew up, they founded a town at the spot where their basket had landed. But the brothers quarreled, and Romulus killed Remus. He named the new town Rome, after himself. He later disappeared, and it is said he turned into a god.

In the 1970s, a movement began to protect the remaining wolves, and their population is now rising. Wolves no longer live in the Italian Alps or in Sicily, but the Apennines are now home to an estimated five hundred to six hundred wolves.

Ibex live high in the Alps. Some live at elevations of higher than 2 miles (3 km).

European ibex and chamois, both goatlike antelopes, live in the Alps. Both animals are rare. Wild boars and foxes are more common. Small rodents such as voles and mice abound, in both the suburbs and the countryside.

The chamois has a smooth, reddish-brown coat in the summer and a thick, dark brown coat in the winter.

About five hundred species of birds live in Italy or pass through on their annual migrations. Large birds such as eagles, hawks, vultures, and falcons live in the mountains. Other birds found in Italy range from dramatic spoonbills and ibises to tiny warblers.

The golden eagle was once common throughout Europe. The mountains of Italy are among the few places left in Europe where they live.

Italy is also home to more than a dozen snake species, including three species of poisonous vipers. Lizards such as geckos, Italian wall lizards, and three-toed skinks scurry across the land, while tree frogs, common toads, and many other amphibians linger near streams and ponds.

The four-lined snake is one of Europe's largest snakes. It can grow to a length of 6 feet (2 m).

National Parks

Italy has established several national parks to protect the natural world and the animals that live there. Gran Paradiso National Park spreads across a high mountain near the French border. Originally a royal hunting preserve, it is now Italy's oldest national park. Chamois and ibex live in its forests of larch and fir and its mountain grasslands. The park also has a permanent glacier.

The mountainous Gran Paradiso National Park lies in northwestern Italy. Its highest peak rises 13,323 feet (4,061 m) above sea level.

Two national parks lie in the Apennines, east of Rome. Abruzzo National Park is wild mountain country, one of the rare places in Italy where wolves and bears still roam. Majella National Park is larger and even wilder than Abruzzo. Wild

Abruzzo National Park is home to many of Italy's protected species.

boars, wolves, brown bears, and roe deer live in its forests. Chamois live on the high meadows. Otters swim in the rivers that run through the mountain park. Many birds pass through these parks in the spring and fall. These include the lanner, a type of falcon, and the golden eagle, which is almost extinct in other parts of Europe.

Foxes are common in Abruzzo National Park and throughout the Italian countryside.

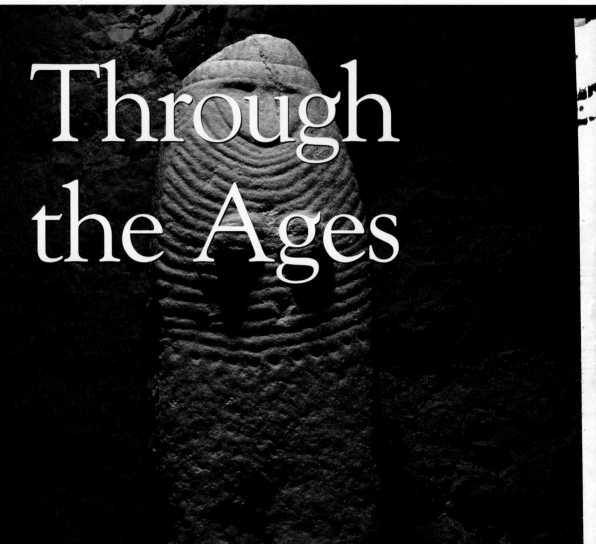

Through the Ages

HE FIRST PEOPLE TO LIVE IN WHAT IS NOW ITALY WERE hunters. Prehistoric people who lived in the valleys of what is now northern Italy left many petroglyphs, or carvings in rock. An area of northern Italy called Val Camonica contains about 350,000 petroglyphs created some ten thousand years ago. Some of the petroglyphs show hunting scenes. Others depict people and even maps.

In time, the people who lived on the Italian peninsula began to breed livestock. The name *Italy* comes from the word *italia*, meaning "calf land." The region's early people are called Italic.

Opposite: **This ancient marble figure of a mother was uncovered near Arco in northeastern Italy.**

These petroglyphs were made in the area called Val Camonica more than two thousand years ago.

The city of Populonia was a center for ironworking in the ancient Etruscan civilization.

Many different peoples stopped in Italy while traveling on the Mediterranean Sea. Villages grew along lakes and rivers. People learned to work with pottery and glass. By approximately four thousand years ago, they had gathered into tribes with different languages and customs. Italy's mountains and broken coastlines made it difficult for the tribes to communicate with one another, and the groups remained isolated.

The Etruscans

In the central part of Italy, one of these groups, the Etruscans, developed a powerful civilization by about 800 B.C. Their homeland was called Etruria. Little is known about the Etruscans, in part because few of their written records survived. Their language does not seem to resemble any known language. Its alphabet, however, is similar to the Greek alphabet.

At the height of their civilization, the Etruscans had twelve major cities. They built roads and drained swamps to make usable land. Archaeological evidence shows that Etruscans spent a lot of time relaxing and eating. They also loved art and used metal. Some Etruscan sculptures from 2,500 years ago have survived and can be seen today. Etruscan women had high status and, unlike women in many other ancient civilizations, could own property.

The Coming of the Greeks

The southern part of the Italian boot is close to Greece, and several Greek cultures influenced the cultures of Italy. People from the Greek city of Corinth settled on Sicily. Starting about 734 B.C., they built a city called Syracuse on the island's east coast. The Greeks ruled this city, and the Sicilians were enslaved.

The Greeks established other cities on the mainland, in a cluster known as Magna Graecia, which means "Great Greece" in Latin, the language of ancient Rome. A later Greek city, called Poseidonia after Poseidon, the Greek god of the sea, flourished in about 550 B.C. When Italic people conquered the city, which was located south of Naples, they changed its name to Paestum. The ruins of Greek temples there are among the best-preserved Greek structures anywhere.

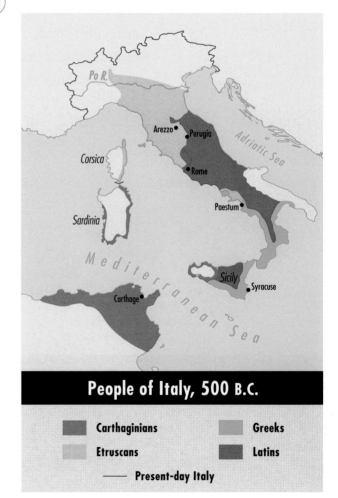

People of Italy, 500 B.C.

| | Carthaginians | | Greeks |
| | Etruscans | | Latins |

—— Present-day Italy

The Making of an Empire

A group of people called Latins built villages south of the Tiber River in central Italy. Their name comes from Latium, the name of a nearby plain. Rome, one of the Latin towns, was located on the border between Latium and Etruria.

Neither the Greeks nor the Etruscans paid much attention to the growth of Rome, possibly because the Latin people mixed bits of Greek and Etruscan culture with their own. The Latins also made innovations. They developed a central government that oversaw all their cities, something that neither the Greeks nor the Etruscans had. This central government, headquartered in Rome, soon made Rome the leading city of the western Mediterranean.

At first, kings led Rome, but in 509 B.C., Rome became a republic. In this form of government, people elect government officials. Two elected officials called consuls ruled Rome. The consuls were also military leaders. They were later assisted by an advisory council called the Senate, which was made up of citizens from wealthy families. Other advisers, called tribunes, came from among the common people and the military.

Rome soon began taking over surrounding communities, and by about

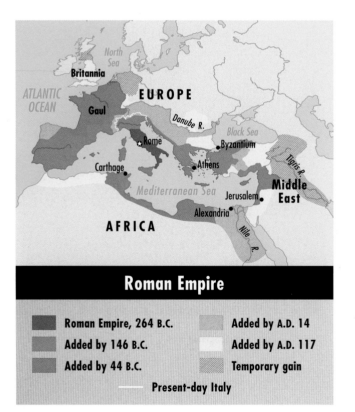

Roman Empire

- Roman Empire, 264 B.C.
- Added by 146 B.C.
- Added by 44 B.C.
- Added by A.D. 14
- Added by A.D. 117
- Temporary gain
- —— Present-day Italy

Fabulous Feats of Engineering

By about 300 B.C., as many as 150,000 people may have been living in Rome. Romans relied on superb engineering skills to make their city function well. They built aqueducts to bring water to the city. Stone, leather, and wooden pipes carried water underground from mountainsides as far as 50 miles (80 km) away. In some places, high arches (left) supported pipes that carried water across valleys.

The Romans built great roads that their armies used. The Appian Way ran in a straight line from Rome to Naples. The road surface of tightly fitting stones curved to allow rainwater to drain off. The road was so well built that people still use some parts of it.

200 B.C., the Romans controlled most of Italy. As they expanded their territory, the Romans also spread their language, and soon people across Italy were speaking Latin.

Once in control of Italy, the Romans began to look southward across the Mediterranean Sea. In a series of wars called the Punic Wars, the Romans conquered the city of Carthage in North Africa, where Tunisia now lies. To the west, they conquered Gaul, which included most of western Europe, as well as Britannia (England). They also spread eastward through the Middle East.

Elephants in the Alps

Hannibal was a general in Carthage during the Second Punic War. He was determined to defeat the Romans. Because the Romans ruled the sea, Hannibal sought an overland route to attack Rome. For four months during the winter of 218–217 B.C., he led an estimated forty thousand soldiers, their horses, and many pack elephants on a march through Spain and across the Alps. Finally, Hannibal's exhausted forces descended into the plains of northern Italy.

Hannibal's men conquered much of northern Italy, but though they fought for years, they never took Rome. When Roman general Scipio Africanus attacked Carthage itself, Hannibal was forced to return to North Africa. In 202 B.C., Scipio's troops defeated Hannibal's.

Not all people were regarded as citizens and given the right to vote in the Roman Republic. Many people were enslaved. Male Roman citizens were expected to be soldiers, so the Romans brought enslaved people from conquered lands to work Italian farms. A slave named Spartacus led a massive uprising that Roman soldiers put down in 72 B.C. Later, when Roman power deteriorated, the slaves were freed.

The Emperors

Julius Caesar is often called an emperor, which is a sole leader of an empire, but in fact he was not. He was the senior consul, and thus dictator, of Rome. He served from 49 to 44 B.C., when he was murdered by his competitors. Julius Caesar was memorialized by later Roman leaders, who called themselves caesars. Under the caesars, Rome was no longer a republic. The caesars were said to be gods after their deaths.

In 27 B.C., Octavian, the great-nephew of Julius Caesar, changed his name to Augustus Caesar and declared himself the first Roman emperor. Augustus ruled for more than forty years and established a dynasty, or ruling family, which built Rome into a grand city.

Augustus, the first Roman emperor, ruled from 27 B.C. to A.D. 14.

Cleopatra, Murder, and Suicide

In 48 B.C., Rome was involved in a civil war that spilled into Egypt. There, Julius Caesar met and fell in love with Cleopatra, who, along with her brother, ruled Egypt. She may have loved Caesar, too, but she also used his

power to keep herself on the throne. He helped her win a civil war and probably fathered her son.

After Julius Caesar and Cleopatra returned to Rome, Caesar was soon murdered. Mark Antony, Caesar's second in command, also fell in love with the Egyptian queen. But Antony and Octavian were vying for power, so Antony married Octavian's sister for political reasons. Octavian became Augustus Caesar.

Later, Antony traveled to Egypt, where he married Cleopatra. Antony gave Cleopatra whatever she wanted, even Roman provinces. Octavian could not accept that, and in 31 B.C., Antony's and Octavian's naval forces clashed in the Battle of Actium. When Cleopatra withdrew her own forces from the battle, Octavian easily defeated Antony. Seeing no future, Antony committed suicide. Rather than see Octavian on her Egyptian throne, Cleopatra, too, took her own life.

The End of Empire

The Roman Empire reached its greatest scope and power in about A.D. 200, but even then it was beginning to weaken. Hoping to help stabilize the empire, Emperor Diocletian split it into four smaller sections. The two eastern sections were headquartered in Byzantium—now Istanbul, Turkey. The two western sections were still headquartered in Rome. In 324, however, Constantine, the senior eastern leader, took over the entire empire. He became a Christian and turned the empire into a Christian state. Constantine changed the name of Byzantium. He named it Constantinople, after himself, and made it the capital of the empire.

This 1622 oil sketch by painter Peter Paul Rubens depicts Constantine (in red) directing the construction of the city of Constantinople.

The Ostrogoths attacked the city of Perugia in 547. The city was entirely destroyed.

The Roman Empire continued to weaken and suffered frequent invasions by Germanic tribes from the north. In 410, the Visigoths sacked Rome. The Huns, led by Attila, invaded in 452. The Vandals finished the empire off a few years later. Rome and the western empire were gone.

Starting in 488, the Ostrogoths, a people from western Russia, conquered other parts of the Italian peninsula and held their territory for several decades. The Ostrogoth wars left many towns and villages in ruins.

For many centuries thereafter, Italy was broken into small kingdoms and city-states. The Lombards, another Germanic tribe, invaded in the 500s. For more than two hundred years, they held the northern regions now called Lombardy and Tuscany. Several cities, including Milan, developed under the Lombards. Meanwhile, Rome became an independent papal state, meaning it was owned by the pope, the leader of the Roman Catholic Church. Venice and Naples both achieved independence during this period, becoming powerful city-states.

After declaring himself head of the Holy Roman Empire, Charlemagne dramatically increased the empire's power and size.

In 800, Charlemagne, the king of a German people called the Franks, captured Lombardy. In Rome, the pope declared Charlemagne emperor of the Holy Roman Empire. From that time on, European kings saw it as part of their holy duty to preserve the pope and his territories in Rome.

For the next thousand years, German kings used the title Holy Roman Emperor. Sometimes there was an actual empire that included lands in northern and central Italy, but more often there wasn't. It was simply a title German kings used because of alliances they formed with the popes.

Events in Sicily

In the 800s, while the Franks were busy in the north, Arabs crossed the Mediterranean from Africa and conquered Sicily. They made Palermo their capital. From there, they spread to the Italian peninsula. Troops from Constantinople forced them off the mainland, but the Arabs retained control of Sicily and Sardinia for a hundred years. Then, in 1060, people from France called Normans conquered Sicily.

For part of the twelfth century, Sicily was the wealthiest state in Europe. Roger II, Sicily's Norman king, claimed both the island and all land on the Italian peninsula south of Naples. French and Spanish kings also laid claim to Sicily. In 1443, Alfonso V, king of Aragon (a region in Spain), claimed both Sicily and Naples on the mainland and called his land the Kingdom of the Two Sicilies.

The Venetian Republic

Venice, the island city, did not exist during the height of the Roman Empire. But by 1100, it had become a thriving city-state that controlled the Adriatic coastline. It became the busiest port city in the world, serving as a midway point between Asia and Europe. Goods shipped from one to the other made a stop in Venice's warehouses.

Venice also became an awesome military power. It produced warships in huge numbers. Many ships heading to the Middle East to fight wars left from Venice.

The arrival in the Americas of Christopher Columbus, an explorer from Genoa, Italy, who was working for Spain,

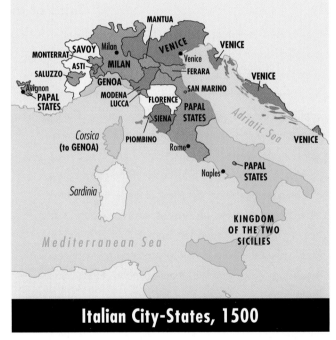

Italian City-States, 1500

The Theft of a Saint

The patron saint of Venice is Saint Mark, or San Marco, an early follower of Jesus who helped spread his message. Mark was killed and buried in Alexandria, Egypt, in A.D. 57. In 829, two Venetian merchants stole his remains and took them to Venice for reburial in order to bring their church prestige. A large church called the Basilica of San Marco was built over the burial site of Saint Mark's remains. The basilica is a fantasy of gold and mosaics and onion-shaped domes. Saint Mark's symbol, the winged lion, is still seen everywhere in Venice.

Tales of the East

Marco Polo (right) was born in 1254 into a Venetian merchant family. His father spent many years in the courts of the Far East. When Marco was seventeen, he accompanied his father and uncle on a trip to the capital of the Mongol Empire, today's Beijing, China. They investigated many lands on the way, often places where no Westerners had ever been before.

Marco Polo grew to adulthood in the royal courts of China. Kublai Khan, the Mongol emperor, delighted in Marco's tales of his travels and probably sent him on missions around his empire. In 1292, Kublai Khan asked the Polo family to accompany a princess to western Asia, and the Venetians were finally able to go home.

Genoa and Venice were often enemies, and during one skirmish, Genoese sailors took Marco Polo prisoner. While in prison—and with the help of fellow prisoner Rustichello da Pisa—he began to write the story of his years in the Far East. The printing press had not yet been invented, so copies of his tale, *The Travels of Marco Polo*, had to be written out by hand. Even so, it became immensely popular.

led to the end of Venice as a great power. European attention now turned to the west and the Americas. Because Venice had no access to the Atlantic Ocean, the city's economy began to decline.

Christopher Columbus left on his first voyage to the Americas in 1492. Here he is shown aboard one of his ships, the *Santa María*.

The Renaissance

After the fall of the Roman Empire, Europe began a period that is called the Middle Ages, or the medieval period. The Middle Ages were dominated by war, illness, and concerns about mortality. During this time, Rome lost much of its former grandeur and vitality. It had perhaps no more than thirteen thousand residents in the 1300s.

Around this time, attitudes began to change. The wealthy began thinking more about human achievement and the world around them. Explorers such as Columbus wanted to find new routes to Asia. Italian churchmen and scholars saw ancient buildings all around them and took an interest in the classical world of Rome and Greece. They began to spend money on beautiful buildings, art, and scholarship. This period came to be called the Renaissance, which means "the Rebirth." It was the rebirth of classical learning after more than a thousand years.

Some of Italy's wealthiest families funded the Renaissance. The Medicis were important in Florence, and one daughter, Catherine, became the queen of France. The Borgias were important in Rome, where they kept their position by murder, treachery, and intrigue. Those families and others built magnificent palaces. They also began to pay to build churches

Galileo and the Church

Galileo Galilei was an Italian scientist born in 1564. In 1608, he learned about the invention of a new device called a telescope. He built one and quickly discovered that Earth's moon was not smooth, as people had thought. Looking farther out into space, he saw that the planet Jupiter had moons orbiting it.

Galileo watched the movement of the planets and realized that the Earth revolved around the Sun. But the Roman Catholic Church insisted that the Earth sat motionless at the center of the universe and that all other bodies, including the Sun, revolved around it. The church told Galileo not to argue that the Earth moved around the Sun. After he wrote a book about it, Galileo was called to Rome to stand trial (right). The church ordered Galileo imprisoned in his house. He continued his scientific work at home until his death in 1642. Only centuries later did the church admit that Galileo had been right.

and make their cities beautiful. Many sculptors and painters became full-time employees of wealthy patrons. Perhaps the greatest artist of them all was Michelangelo, whose patrons included Pope Julius II and the Medici family.

Changing Hands

By the 1700s, Italy was in turmoil. During the previous centuries, the kings of Spain, France, and Austria had controlled different parts of Italy at different times. Sometimes one king would sell a region of Italy to another king. In 1796, France, under Napoléon Bonaparte, took over northern Italy. Napoléon made a deal with Austria, trading parts of Italy, including Venice, for other lands.

Northern Italy became a battlefield time and again. First, the Austrians took it from the French, who then took it back. In 1805, Napoléon was crowned king of the new Kingdom of Italy (consisting of the northern part), and his brother Joseph Bonaparte was later named king of Naples (the southern part). Napoléon pulled Venice into his empire and named his son king of Rome.

By 1815, Napoléon's empire had dissolved, and he was sent into exile on the Italian island of Elba. European leaders met in Austria for the Congress of Vienna, where they again rearranged Europe. Italy ended up split among various nations.

Napoléon Bonaparte's troops march through northern Italy. Napoléon and his brother ruled the region for ten years.

Making a New Kingdom

After the Congress of Vienna, Italy consisted primarily of the Kingdom of Sardinia (part of northern Italy and Sardinia) and the Kingdom of Naples (most of southern Italy plus Sicily). In between were the Papal States (primarily Rome). Austria controlled Venice and much of northern Italy.

In the south, a secret society called Carboneria (meaning "charcoal burners") sought a constitution that would give the people some power. The society's aims quickly spread throughout the Italian boot. The idea of political change gained momentum.

Garibaldi, the Italian Hero

A sea captain named Giuseppe Garibaldi (1807–1882) thought Italians should rule their own land as a republic. After leading an uprising in 1834 that failed, he was forced into exile in South America. Fourteen years later, Conte (Count) Camillo Benso di Cavour, prime minister of the Kingdom of Sardinia, invited Garibaldi back and made him a general. Without the approval of either Victor Emmanuel II (the king of Sardinia) or Cavour, Garibaldi collected a thousand followers and set sail for Sicily, where the people had suffered in poverty for many years.

Garibaldi's army freed the Sicilians and then moved across the Strait of Messina and north to Naples. He declared himself dictator of southern Italy and Sicily but served only long enough for people to vote in favor of the new Kingdom of Italy under King Victor Emmanuel II.

People began to think and write about the possibility that there was, in fact, a genuinely Italian people, and that they didn't have to always be bossed around by outsiders. This movement is called the Risorgimento, meaning "Reawakening" or "Rising Again." Its most popular leader was Giuseppe Garibaldi, who is sometimes called "the Father of Modern Italy."

After many years of rebellions and wars, the new nation called the Kingdom of Italy was formed. It united Italy, north and south, for the first time since the days of the Roman Empire. On March 17, 1861, Italy's first parliament met. It proclaimed the nation a constitutional monarchy with Victor Emmanuel II as the king.

It wasn't easy becoming a nation. The people who had fought for their own country were still, for the most part, quite poor. The quick changes in life that they had hoped for did not come to pass. During the first decades of Italian government, millions of Italians left to find better lives elsewhere. Many went to the United States.

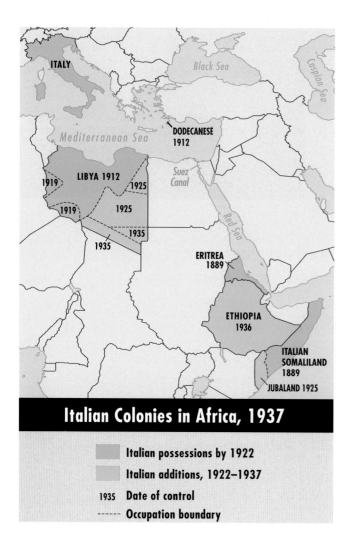

Italian Colonies in Africa, 1937

Italian possessions by 1922

Italian additions, 1922–1937

1935   Date of control

------   Occupation boundary

A Colonial Power

In 1869, the Suez Canal opened. This waterway cut across Egypt, connecting the Mediterranean to the Red Sea, an arm of the Indian Ocean. Boats could now reach eastern Africa easily from Europe. In the late 1800s, European nations raced to claim land and form colonies in Africa. Italian nationalists wanted glory for their country; they wanted to rebuild the Roman Empire. Italy took over Somaliland and Eritrea in East Africa. Italy tried to conquer Ethiopia as well, but Ethiopian troops defeated the Italians. This was a huge embarrassment for Italy.

To satisfy the nationalists, in 1911, Italy invaded Libya in North Africa. By 1912, Italy had taken control of Libya. The Italian military killed any Arabs who resisted their control.

The Fascist Era

In 1915, Italy joined forces with Great Britain, France, and Russia to fight Germany and Austria-Hungary in World War I. Treaties signed at the end of the war gave Italy the northern regions of Trentino and Alto Adige, which had belonged to Austria. But the price was high. A half million Italians died in the war.

The postwar era was a time of turmoil. With a poor economy and prices rising quickly, workers' strikes were common. Some people wanted Italy to adopt communism, a political system in which the government owns most businesses and controls the economy. Armed groups that believed in nationalism, militarism, and order opposed the communists. They became known as fascists. Fascists fought communists in cities throughout Italy.

In 1922, fascist leader Benito Mussolini took control of the country. Mussolini soon became a dictator. In the coming years, he censored the press and banned all political parties but his own. He stripped parliament of power, and his decrees gained the force of law.

The fascists wanted to create an Italian empire. In the 1930s, fascist Italy tried again to capture Ethiopia. The Italians succeeded, but at great cost. During the invasion, the Italians used mustard gas and other chemical weapons on the Ethiopians.

Benito Mussolini toured the cities of Italy to gain support for his fascist regime. Here, he addresses a crowd in Pistoia in 1930.

In some cases, Italian troops killed all Ethiopian civilians they came across. The Italians occupied Ethiopia until 1941. During that period, more than four hundred thousand Ethiopians were killed and another three hundred thousand died of hunger.

World War II

During the 1930s, Adolf Hitler, also a fascist leader, had come to power in Germany. Mussolini and Hitler were soon cooperating. Hitler had enacted many laws persecuting Jewish people and others. Likewise, in 1938 Mussolini enacted racial laws, banning Jewish people from attending public schools, having government jobs, or owning large businesses.

At the beginning of World War II, Adolf Hitler and Benito Mussolini were allies. In this photograph, the two leaders inspect the Italian Guard of Honor in Venice.

World War II began in 1939, after Germany invaded Poland. The following year, Italy and Germany formed an alliance. Their alliance, called the Axis, would later include Japan. During World War II, the Axis powers fought the Allies—Britain, France, the Soviet Union (which has since split apart into many different countries, including Russia), the United States, Canada, and many other nations around the world.

Italian troops joined German troops as Hitler's forces moved through Europe, taking over country after country. Italian soldiers rushed home when Allied troops landed in Sicily in July 1943. The Allies began fighting their way up the Italian boot. For the first time in years, the Italian government took a step not approved by Mussolini—they dismissed him from his position. He was arrested and imprisoned in the mountains. German troops helped him escape, and he formed a government in the north that was controlled by Germany.

A soldier digs a foxhole during the Allied invasion of Sicily in 1943. The battle for Sicily lasted more than a month, and the Allied victory led to the invasion of the Italian mainland.

As the Allies fought their way north, Italian resistance fighters fought Mussolini's supporters in what became a civil war. In April 1945, Mussolini was caught in northern Italy while trying to escape to Austria. He was shot, and his body was hung upside down in a square in Milan where many antifascists had been executed. The following month, World War II ended in Europe.

The New Republic

Italy had been a dictatorship for years. At the war's end, it was unclear what shape the new Italian government would take. On June 2, 1946, an election was held to decide. For the first time, women voted along with men. The vote was 54 percent in favor of setting up a republic rather than returning to a monarchy. Only 46 percent wanted to have a king again.

The strongest political parties of the new Italian republic were the Christian Democrats and the Communists. The first prime minister, Alcide de Gasperi of the Christian Democrats, remained in office until 1953. In those years, the nation's economy began to grow. Highways and houses were built, and Italy became a major manufacturing nation.

Terrorism died down in the 1980s but did not end entirely. In 1984, a bomb exploded on a train traveling from Naples to Bologna, killing seventeen and injuring hundreds.

Terrorism

Political and social conflicts grew violent in the late 1960s and the 1970s. Neofascists ("new fascists") wanted to make the country less stable so that fascists could regain power. Some of them carried out random bombings beginning in 1969. In the coming years, communists and anarchists (people opposed to government and authority) also committed terrorist acts.

One active terrorist group in this period was the Red Brigades, whose members wanted to make Italy a communist nation. They used kidnapping, murder, and bombings to draw attention to their cause. In 1978, they kidnapped and murdered Aldo Moro, a former prime minister of Italy. After this, they lost a great deal of support.

In 1980, eighty-four people died in a bomb blast in the Bologna train station. The bombing was blamed on neofascists. Then, as the decade progressed, terrorism died down.

A New Era

In the 1980s, organized crime activity increased. Political corruption was also a problem. In 1992, several political figures were charged with corruption. These politicians informed authorities about other people, and they in turn informed on others. Eventually, more than seven hundred people were charged with crimes. This anticorruption program was officially called Operation Clean Hands. As a result of the scandal, the Christian Democratic Party and several other parties dissolved in the early 1990s. In the next few years, voters approved reforms aimed at improving the government and limiting corruption.

In 1994, a conservative named Silvio Berlusconi became prime minister. Berlusconi is a billionaire who owns several television stations and many newspapers, as well as A.C. Milan, a prominent soccer team. Berlusconi soon fell from power, but he became prime minister again in 2001, pledging to cut taxes and stimulate the economy. Although he managed to stay in office for five years, he made little progress. And like many other Italian politicians, he was accused of corruption.

Despite the political upheavals, Italy has thrived. By 2008, it had the world's seventh-largest economy. Each year, millions of tourists flock to the country to enjoy its magnificent scenery and fantastic art.

Silvio Berlusconi is the third-richest person in Italy.

Governing the Republic

REPUBBLICA ITALIANA IS THE OFFICIAL NAME OF THE Italian Republic. Its constitution, which went into effect in 1948, divides the government into three parts: legislative, executive, and judicial.

Opposite: **Quirinale Palace in Rome is the official residence of the president. It was built as a summer home for Pope Gregory XII in the late 1500s.**

The Legislative Branch

The legislative branch is the lawmaking part of government. The Italian legislature, or parliament, has two houses. The lower house is the Chamber of Deputies. Citizens living in Italy who

The Italian Senate meets for a vote in 2008.

are at least eighteen years old elect its 630 members to five-year terms. Italians who live in other countries elect twelve deputies.

Voters who are at least twenty-five years old elect the 315 members of the upper house, the Senate, to five-year terms. Italians living abroad elect six senators. In addition to the elected senators, a few senators serve for life. Most are former presidents.

NATIONAL GOVERNMENT OF ITALY

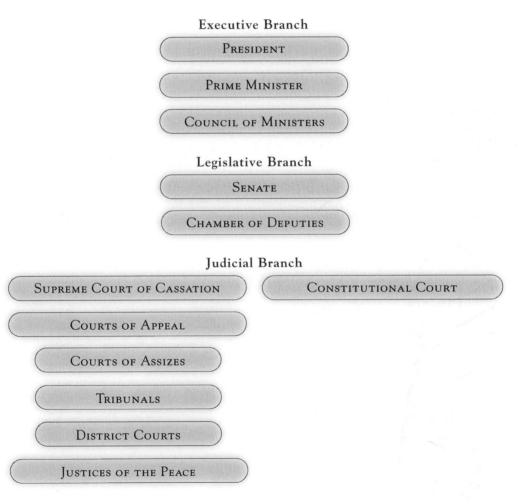

Executive Branch

PRESIDENT

PRIME MINISTER

COUNCIL OF MINISTERS

Legislative Branch

SENATE

CHAMBER OF DEPUTIES

Judicial Branch

SUPREME COURT OF CASSATION

CONSTITUTIONAL COURT

COURTS OF APPEAL

COURTS OF ASSIZES

TRIBUNALS

DISTRICT COURTS

JUSTICES OF THE PEACE

The president lives and works at Quirinale Palace.

The Executive Branch

The legislature and representatives from the regions elect Italy's president, who is the chief of state. The president holds office for a seven-year term. Unlike the U.S. president, the Italian president has little to do with running the government.

The head of the government is, instead, the prime minister, who is appointed by the president. The prime minister usually heads the party that holds the most seats in the Chamber of Deputies. Prime ministers keep their jobs only as long as they have the support of the parliament. If a prime minister loses a

Many politicians attended the swearing-in ceremony of Prime Minister Romano Prodi. Like many prime ministers, Prodi served only a short time in office.

confidence vote in the parliament, he or she must step down. Elections follow, and a new prime minister is named.

A cabinet, the Council of Ministers, assists the prime minister. The ministers run various departments such as foreign affairs, public works, and health.

The Judicial Branch

The judicial branch includes courts at several levels. Local justices of the peace handle simple civil (noncriminal) matters. Their decisions can be appealed to the district courts, where judges handle both civil and criminal matters. Several judicial districts report to a tribunal, and from tribunals, cases go to the twenty-three courts of appeal.

Major criminal cases are tried before courts of assizes. They have their own systems of appeals to the highest court, called the Supreme Court of Cassation. *Cassation* means the power to cancel other courts' decisions.

A different high court is the Constitutional Court, which has fifteen members appointed for nine-year terms. They make sure legislation does not contradict the constitution. The Constitutional Court also handles conflicts between regions.

A judge in Milan announces a ruling.

Political Parties

In Italy, citizens vote for political parties rather than for individuals. Each party then gets a certain number of seats in the

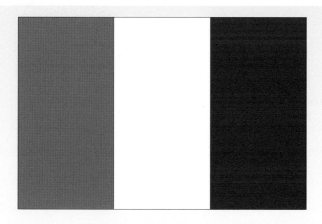

Italy's Flag

The Italian flag has three vertical stripes of green, white, and red. It has been used since before Italy became a unified nation. The red and white came from the flag of Milan, and the green from the color of uniforms in Lombardy. The flag was officially adopted in 1946. Earlier versions included a shield in the middle of the white stripe.

Silvio Berlusconi, the leader of the Forza Party, talks with lawmakers prior to a vote.

parliament based on the percentage of the vote it received. This is called proportional representation. Under this system, even small political parties are represented in the parliament.

The National Anthem

Goffredo Mameli wrote the lyrics to Italy's national anthem, "Il Conti degli Italiani" ("The Song of the Italians"), in 1847. The music is by Michele Novaro.

Italian lyrics	English translation
Fratelli d'Italia	*Italian brothers,*
L'Italia s'è desta,	*Italy has arisen,*
Dell'elmo di Scipio	*With Scipio's helmet*
S'è cinta la testa.	*binding her head.*
Dov'è la Vittoria?	*Where is Victory?*
Le porga la chioma,	*Let her bow down,*
Ché schiava di Roma	*For God has made her*
Iddio la creò.	*The slave of Rome.*
Stringiamci a coorte,	*Let us gather in legions,*
Siam pronti alla morte!	*Ready to die!*
L'Italia chiamò!	*Italy has called!*

A coalition (partnership) of two or more political parties often runs Italy's government. Italy has so many political parties that without coalitions, no party would have enough votes to win the right to rule. Romano Prodi became prime minister in 2006 because ten different parties joined forces.

Since 2005, the coalition that obtains the most votes has received extra seats in the Chamber of Deputies, bringing their number up to a minimum of 340 seats. The hope is that this will make the government more stable. Under the new rules, a party also has to receive a certain percentage of the vote to be represented. Parties that are part of a coalition must receive at least 2 percent of the vote, stand-alone parties must receive 4 percent, and coalitions as a whole must receive 10 percent.

Over the years, coalitions have come and gone. Each time a coalition fell apart, a new government had to be formed. In the first fifty years of modern Italy, the average government lasted only eleven months.

Mustapha Mansouri, president of the Immigrant Party, stands in front of the parliament building in 2007.

In 2006, Italians gathered in a Rome square awaiting the results of elections that determined who controlled the parliament.

To outsiders, Italy sometimes looked unstable. Some people believed that nothing ever got done because the government changed all the time. But in reality, a few government officials who had been in positions of power for a long time made most decisions. These officials actually had more power than the parliament or the cabinet. Many of these long-time officials were charged with corruption in Operation Clean Hands.

Local Government

Italy is divided into twenty regions, each governed by a regional council elected by the people. The regions are composed of ninety-five provinces, which are themselves divided into communes (municipalities or towns). Local governments run the approximately 8,100 communes.

A Voice of Outrage

Many Italians do not trust their government. They believe that many government officials are corrupt. Beppe Grillo is Italy's most popular comedian—and the most popular blogger in Italy. He has become the public voice of rage at political corruption and waste. In 2007, he pointed out that there were twenty-four convicted criminals in Italy's parliament. Italian lawmakers have voted to make themselves the best-paid legislators in Europe—their salary is almost four times that of Spanish legislators. Italian lawmakers have also voted to give themselves many other benefits. They are driven around in Europe's largest fleet of chauffeured cars, and they receive free air travel and free tennis lessons. Beppo speaks for many Italians when he says, "The whole kettle of fish stinks to high heaven!"

Rome: Did You Know This?

Rome is often called the Eternal City. The spirits of ancient civilizations live on in monuments and ruins that are located throughout the city. Yet Rome today is also a vibrant, modern city. Once the capital of a huge empire, Rome has been the capital of Italy since 1871.

Rome is located in the central part of the Italian boot along the Tiber River. The city was once defined by the Seven Hills of Rome. Today, these hills are in the center of a sprawling city, which is home to more than 2.5 million people. Palatine Hill is rich in ancient ruins and medieval mansions. Another of the Seven Hills, Capitoline, was the site of the Roman government in ancient times, as it is today. Michelangelo designed many structures on the Capitoline. In a valley among the Seven Hills lies

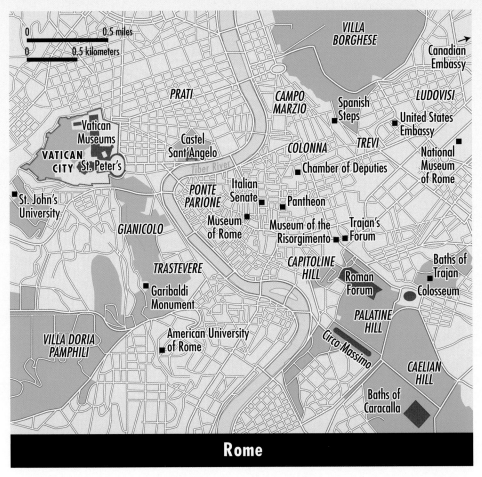

Rome

the Forum (above), the center of ancient Rome, an area surrounded by temples and palaces.

Rome also thrived during the Renaissance, when cities all over Italy competed to have the greatest art and architecture. Many of the city's great churches and fountains were built during the Renaissance.

Italy at Work

In Florence, a street musician plays for a crowd of tourists.

FOR THE FIRST HALF OF THE TWENTIETH CENTURY, ITALY'S economy lagged behind those of other European countries. But in the middle of the twentieth century, industry blossomed. Italy also became one of the world's top tourist destinations. Today, Italy has the world's seventh-largest economy.

Tourism

Tourism is the largest segment of the Italian economy. Millions of Italians work in the tourist industry. They work in hotels and restaurants. They drive taxis and lead tour groups.

Tourists flock to Italy for its gorgeous scenery, beautiful weather, and incredible art. Italy is the fifth most visited nation in the world, welcoming about forty million tourists each year.

Opposite: **Some people in Venice make a living as gondoliers, transporting tourists on the city's canals in boats called gondolas.**

Beach umbrellas provide shade on a bright Sicilian beach. People travel to Italy from all over Europe to enjoy the sun and water.

One major destination is the Italian Riviera, which draws visitors with its beautiful beaches, sunny days, and cool nights. Many tourists head to Rome to see its ancient ruins and magnificent art. Tuscany is also rich in art and appealing landscapes. Twenty million people travel to Venice every year to experience the charms of a city that has canals instead of roads.

Agriculture

About one-third of Italy is used for agriculture. In the middle of the twentieth century, half the Italian workforce was employed in agriculture. Today, only 4 percent works in agriculture.

In the south, olive trees are at the center of the agriculture industry. In the past, people burned oil from the olives in small lamps to make light. Today, olive oil is the base ingredient in much Italian cooking. In some parts of Italy, nets on the ground catch ripe olives as they fall from the trees. Growers collect them and then press them for their oil. Italy and Spain are the world's two main producers of olives.

Italy also grows abundant grapes, primarily to make wine. Italy is second only to France in the production of wine. The main vineyard area is Tuscany.

Other important crops in Italy include grains, sugar beets, and fruits. Most hard, or durum, wheat, which is used to make pasta, grows in the south. Wheat used for breads and other baked goods, including pizza crust, grows in the north. Fruits grown in Italy include apples, oranges, peaches, figs, and dates.

Italy's dairy herds in the northern part of the country provide the milk for making cheeses such as parmesan and mozzarella, which are

Resources

Corn and wheat	Al	Aluminum	K Potash
Fruit and vegetables	Bx	Bauxite	Mn Manganese
Forests	C	Coal	NG Natural gas
Grapes and wine	Cem	Cement	⚒ Oil
Livestock ranching	Clay	Clay	Pb Lead
Nonagricultural land	Fe	Iron ore	Salt Salt
	Feld	Feldspar	Zn Zinc

used in many Italian dishes. Dozens of kinds of cheeses are made in Italy.

Mining

Mining is not a major industry in Italy. The country's most valuable resource is natural gas, which is found in the Po Valley and the Adriatic Sea. Italy also has some oil. Most of the oil wells are in the south. Miners dig for feldspar, talc, lead, salt, and lignite in Italy.

Industry

Italy's economy has changed dramatically since the middle of the twentieth century. At that time, it was based on agriculture, and many people were poor. Today, Italy has one of the world's largest economies. What changed?

What Italy Grows, Makes, and Mines

Agriculture (2005)

Sugar beets	14,000,000 metric tons
Grapes	8,554,000 metric tons
Wheat	7,717,000 metric tons

Manufacturing

Steel (2004)	15,200,000 metric tons
Motor vehicles (2004)	1,272,000 units
Wine (2003)	4, 409,000 metric tons

Mining (2004)

Natural gas	11,490,000,000 cubic meters
Oil	53,000,000 barrels
Feldspar	2,500,000 metric tons

The answer is that during those years, Italy began importing materials from all over the world and making them into goods that the world, in turn, wanted to buy. This "value-added" work happens in many small- and medium-sized companies—often owned by families—located all over the country, though primarily in the north. These firms produce clothing, leather shoes, ceramic items, mechanical goods, and much more. In recent years, however, many small, family-owned businesses have had a hard time competing with businesses outside of Europe. Companies in countries such as China pay their workers less, so they can charge less for their products. Still, Italy remains a leading producer of clothing, food products, machinery, steel, and furniture.

A worker adjusts the displays in the shop at a wool factory in Stia, a town in Tuscany. Italy has long produced high-quality textiles and clothing.

The Billion-Dollar Designer

Giorgio Armani (1934–), a native of Piacenza in northern Italy, is a phenomenon in the fashion world. His designs emphasize sophisticated elegance. His Giorgio perfume is one of the most popular scents in the world. A/X (Armani Exchange) sells casual clothes aimed at younger people. It has been estimated that Armani's enterprises, which are headquartered in Milan, are worth almost US$2 billion.

The center of Italian industry is in the north. Milan is the nation's industrial capital, renowned for many different industries. Milan is also Italy's design capital—smart, chic, and trendy. Its fashion houses include Benetton, Gucci, Prada, Valentino, and Versace. The international publishing firms of Rizzoli and Mondadori have their headquarters in Milan. An international furniture show in Milan attracts more than two thousand firms from 140 countries. Pirelli makes tires and other rubber products there. In the nearby town of Gardone Val Trompia, Beretta has been making firearms for almost five centuries. Italy's aerospace industry, centered in Milan, has been growing for many years. Milan is the financial capital of Italy, too. The Italian stock exchange and many international banks are located there.

Genoa and Turin are also important industrial cities. Shipbuilding is a leading industry in Genoa. The people of Genoa also produce iron and steel products, motors, and food products.

Fiat makes automobiles and trucks in Turin. The company name stood for Fabbrica Italiana Automobili Torino, meaning "Italian Car Manufacturer of Turin." In the 1950s, Fiat produced an inexpensive model that allowed many Italians and other Europeans to own cars for the first time. Italian sports cars such as Maserati, Lamborghini, Ferrari (which is owned by Fiat), and Alfa Romeo have long been favorites among car lovers.

On narrow Italian streets, pedestrians must always watch out for motor scooters, which can go anywhere. The Vespa motor scooter, made by Piaggio, was first produced in 1946 as

A sports car is assembled at the Ferrari plant in Maranello. The company began as a race-car manufacturer in 1929.

a cheap, quick means of transportation. The Lambretta soon followed. These two convenient scooters became mainstays of young people throughout Europe. Today, Ducati, a Bologna company, is a top motorcycle maker.

The southern half of Italy has less industry than the northern half. Fewer people can find jobs in the south. In some places, the unemployment rate is as high as 25 percent. Over the decades, Italy has poured a great deal of money into the south to try to improve the region's economy, but some Italians say that most of it has gone into the pockets of the politicians.

Money Facts

The lira was the basic unit of Italian currency from 1861, when Italy was unified, to 2002. That year, Italy adopted the euro, the currency of the European Union (EU). Today, fifteen EU states use the euro. One euro is divided into 100 cents. Bills come in values of 5, 10, 20, 50, 100, 200, and 500 euros. Coins come in values of 1 and 2 euros as well as 1, 2, 5, 10, 20, and 50 cents. In 2008, US$1.00 equaled about 0.63 euros, and 1.00 euro equaled US$1.58.

On the front of each euro note is an image of a window or a gateway. On the back is a picture of a bridge. These images do not represent any actual bridges or windows. Instead, they are examples from different historical periods.

Each country designs its own euro coins. Italy chose to honor its greatest artists. Its 2-euro coin shows a portrait by the Renaissance artist Raphael. The 1-euro coin shows a drawing of the human body by Leonardo da Vinci. Other Italian coins show a statue of Emperor Marcus Aurelius and Sandro Botticelli's painting *Birth of Venus*. The 1-cent coin, the smallest, features Castel del Monte, a thirteenth-century castle near Bari.

The European Parliament, which governs the European Union, is located in Brussels, Belgium.

The European Union

In recent decades, Italy established economic partnerships with neighboring countries that have helped it prosper. Italy joined the European Union (EU), a group of twenty-seven nations that work together.

One of the goals of the EU was to establish a single currency. To participate, a country had to prove its economic stability. The Italian government worked hard to reduce the nation's budget deficit—the difference between the amount it spends and the amount it receives. Taxes were increased, and public spending was reduced. These efforts paid off. In 2002, Italy and several other countries began using the euro, the EU currency.

The EU countries have also agreed to a system of free trade. This means that no import taxes are paid on goods shipped between the EU countries. This helps keep the cost of products down.

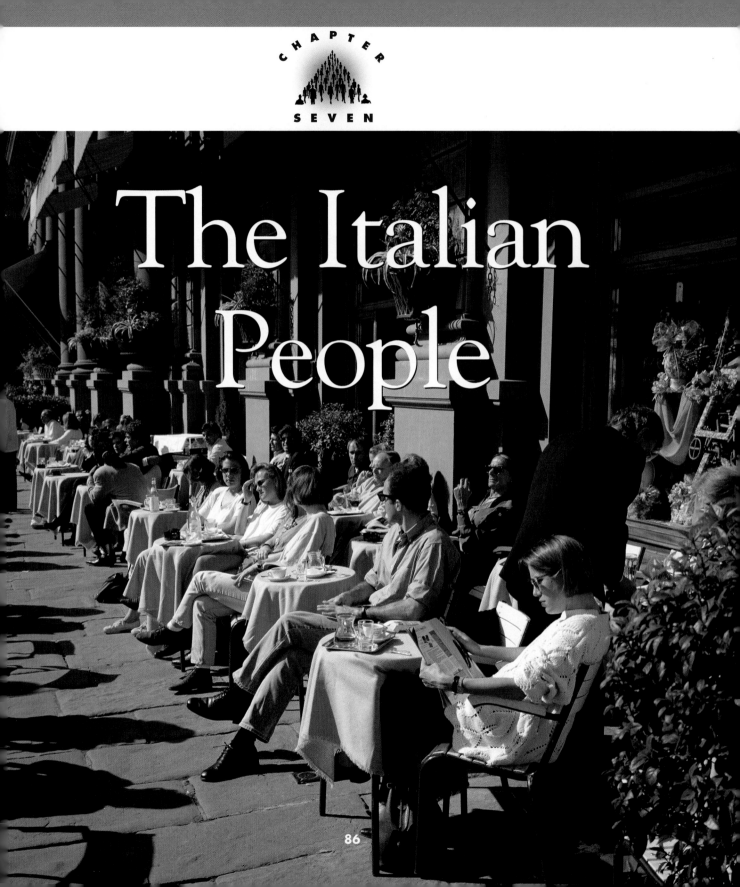

The Italian People

"WITH ITALY MADE, WE MUST NOW MAKE THE Italians." That's what one Italian political leader said after the unification of Italy. A century and a half later, Italy is still trying to make Italians out of people who sometimes seem to feel more loyalty to their own cultural regions than they do to the country as a whole.

People dressed in traditional costumes march in a religious festival in San Lorenzo, in northern Italy.

Population of Major Cities (2007 est.)	
Rome	2,648,000
Milan	1,305,000
Naples	1,047,000
Turin	921,000
Palermo	689,000
Genoa	656,000

Persons per square mile		Persons per square kilometer	
260–517		100–200	
130–259		50–99	
65–129		25–49	
25–64		10–24	
3–24		1–9	
fewer than 3		fewer than 1	

Above right: **The Palermo metropolitan area on the island of Sicily is home to more than 1.3 million people.**

In 2007, Italy's population was estimated at slightly more than fifty-eight million. It is one of the most crowded nations in Europe. Two-thirds of the people live in cities, with the north more urban than the south.

The Newcomers

Immigrants from around the world are eager to enter Italy. In 2007, an estimated 2 immigrants arrived for every 1,000 people already living in Italy. That means an addition of about 120,000 new residents each year.

Immigrants in Italy have come from nearly one hundred nations—everywhere from Ecuador to Senegal. In 2007, an

Who Lives in Italy?	
Italians	93.8%
Other Europeans	3.1%
Africans and Asians	2.5%
Americans	0.6%

Immigrants trying to enter Italy illegally by boat are detained on Lampedusa, an island south of the Italian boot.

estimated 3.7 million legal immigrants lived in Italy, making up 6.2 percent of the population. Half of them are of European origin. Forty percent are African or Asian (primarily from Muslim countries, especially Morocco), and 10 percent are from the Americas. Of the Europeans, the largest group comes from Romania, followed by Albanians and Ukrainians. Many Kurdish people have moved to Italy from Turkey, Iran, and Iraq.

In January 2007, thousands of immigrants gathered in Rome to protest the government's immigration laws.

Italian immigrants wait to be processed at Ellis Island in New York City in 1905.

Leaving Italy

Italians have been involved with North America from the time of Christopher Columbus. In the years when Italy was trying to break away from Austria and other outside control, the authorities forced many revolutionaries to leave the country. Many went to the United States to live.

As the twentieth century began, thousands upon thousands of people left the poverty of southern Italy for a new life across the Atlantic. Between 1850 and 1910, almost five million Italians emigrated to the United States. Most ended up in New York City. Consequently, Italy and the United States have long had close political and emotional ties.

A Different Kind of Immigrant

In the late nineteenth century, hundreds of thousands of Italians moved to the United States. Most were impoverished people from southern Italy trying to find a better life. But Maria Francesca Cabrini was different.

Cabrini was born in the northern region of Lombardy in 1850. She became a nun while still in her twenties and soon founded a new group of nuns called the Missionary Sisters of the Sacred Heart. She hoped to be sent to China to work as a missionary, but instead the pope sent her to the United States.

At first, Mother Cabrini, as she was called, and her nuns worked primarily among Italian immigrants in cities such as New York. Later, they founded sixty-seven hospitals, orphanages, and schools in other crowded cities around the world, including Buenos Aires, Argentina, and Rio de Janeiro, Brazil.

Mother Cabrini became a U.S. citizen in 1909. The Roman Catholic Church declared her a saint in 1946, twenty-nine years after her death. She was the first U.S. citizen to become a saint.

Italian Words and Phrases

si	(see)	yes
no	(no)	no
buon giorno	(bwohn JOHR-noh)	hello; good day
buona sera	(BWOH-nah SEH-rah)	good evening
ciao!	(chow)	hi! (or bye!)
arrivederci	(ah-ree-vuh-DAYR-chi)	good-bye
per favore	(pear fah-VOR-ay)	please
grazie	(GRAH-tsee-ay)	thank you
Come ti chiami?	(KOH-may tee kee-YAH-mee)	What is your name?
Dov'è . . . ?	(doh-VEH)	Where is . . . ?
scusi	(SKOO-zee)	excuse me; sorry

Speaking Italian

Italian is a Romance language, meaning that it is based on Latin, the language of ancient Rome. Spanish, French, Portuguese, and Romanian are also Romance languages. Many people who speak only Spanish can understand and be understood by Italians.

The Italian spoken today originated with Tuscan Italian, a mixture of dialects, or varieties, from the region of Tuscany. In the 1300s, Dante Alighieri wrote *The Divine Comedy* in Tuscan Italian. The leading writers of the Renaissance also used Tuscan Italian.

Although Italian is the nation's main language, several Italian dialects are spoken. These include Friulian, which is spoken by about six hundred thousand people in the northeast of the country, and Sicilian. People in Calabria, the boot's foot, use a dialect that includes a lot of Greek words. These came to the region more than two thousand years ago, when the Greeks colonized the region.

Italian Names

Last names that originated in northern Italy tend to end in *i*, while those from the south often end in *o*. Not all last names in Italy end in vowels. Some have *n* or *s* on the end. The most common Italian surname is Russo.

Religion in Italian Life

A mass is held in Saint Peter's Basilica.

The history of Italy, and especially of Rome, is intertwined with the history of the Roman Catholic Church. Rome became tied to Christianity in the years shortly after Jesus's death. Christians believe that Peter, one of Jesus's closest followers, went to Rome and may have been martyred there, dying for his faith. The Roman Catholic Church says that Saint Peter's Basilica, the church at the Vatican, was built in the fourth century directly over Peter's tomb.

The Early Christians

Roman Christians grew in strength and numbers during the first centuries A.D. Christianity was illegal in the Roman Empire at that time, primarily because Christians believed in

Opposite: **Saint Peter's Basilica is in Vatican City, the center of the Roman Catholic Church. It has one of the tallest domes in the world.**

Religion in Italian Life **95**

Underground Cemeteries

Beneath Rome is an intricate network of underground passageways and chambers that were once used as cemeteries. Called catacombs, they were accessible only by passages leading from the countryside or tunnels within the city. Legend holds that the catacombs were hiding places for Christians in ancient Rome. In more recent times, when European Jews were being persecuted and sent to death camps during World War II, Jewish people hid in the catacombs.

one god. The Romans believed in many gods, and that their own emperors were gods. By the year 200, Christians were being persecuted in Rome. Some Christians were sent into combat against lions in the Colosseum.

Persecution of Christians continued, sometimes brutally, until Emperor Constantine became a Christian. In 313, Constantine announced that Christianity would be tolerated in the Roman Empire. In 330, he decreed that Byzantium (today's Istanbul, Turkey) would be called Constantinople and that it would become the capital of the Roman Empire.

Although no longer the center of the empire, Rome grew in importance to the Christian Church. The Christian Church gradually split into two parts—the Roman Catholic Church, which is headquartered in Rome, and the Orthodox

Church (also called Eastern Orthodox), which doesn't have a headquarters.

The Popes and Rome

From the time of early Christianity, the head of the Catholic Church has been called the pope, from the Latin word *papa*, meaning "father." Throughout most of the church's history, the popes have lived in Rome. For almost one hundred years

The Saint of Assisi

Francesco di Pietro di Bernardone of Assisi, better known as Francis, wanted to be a soldier. But in the year 1205, he had a vision telling him that God had other plans for him. He became a hermit, forsaking all worldly goods. Francis began to preach, drawing followers to his side. He created simple rules by which these men could live as a community under God, trying to live like Jesus. Today, the group he started, called the Franciscans, is one of the largest religious orders in the Catholic Church.

By the time Francis died in 1226, some people believed that he had been an extraordinary man, able to work miracles. Within two years, the church declared him a saint. Saint Francis of Assisi thought that it was the duty of humans to care for the natural world, God's creation. Artists today often depict Saint Francis in paintings and statues with birds and small animals around him.

in the 1300s, the popes moved to Avignon, France, and Rome fell into ruins. During this period, the papacy itself was in danger because of an internal struggle in the church, in which people competed to become pope.

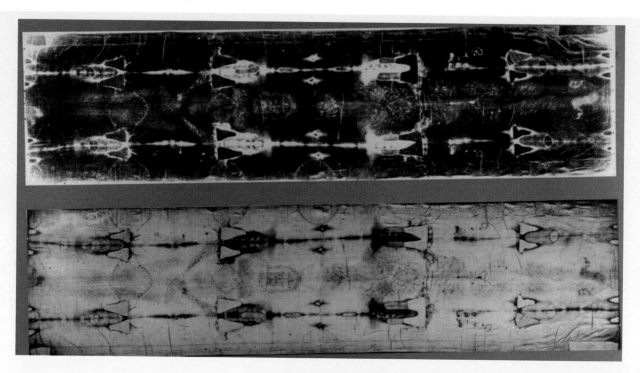

The Shroud of Turin

The Shroud of Turin is an ancient piece of linen cloth that is believed to bear the faint imprint of a male body. Some people believe this cloth once covered the body of Jesus after he was killed. No one knows how the cloth reached Turin, but it has been in the city's San Giovanni Cathedral for at least 420 years.

In the late 1980s, scientists tested a tiny fragment of the cloth to date it by means of carbon-14. Carbon-14 exists in all living things and disappears at a known rate after a living thing dies. The shroud is made of linen from flax plants, so the scientists could determine when the flax died. The scientists concluded that the shroud had been made no earlier than the 1200s. But other scientists argued that the fragments that were tested had been contaminated, making the dating inaccurate. Today, devout Catholics and scientists continue to debate when and how the shroud was created.

Pope Pius IX served as pope from 1846 to 1878. In 1870, he lost control of the Papal States to the Kingdom of Italy.

The End of Papal Control

In the fifteenth century, the Italian popes regained their power and began to use church money to refurbish and beautify Rome. The popes also took firm control of the surrounding territories. The church would hold those lands, called the Papal States, for the next four centuries.

The Papal States lay in the middle of the Italian boot and thus helped keep northern and southern Italy divided. Other Catholic countries sent troops to keep the Papal States from being taken over by neighboring city-states. When the Kingdom of Italy was created in 1861, the Papal States were not included in the new united country. But after French troops withdrew in 1870, a new, free Rome was declared the capital of Italy.

Vatican City

Vatican City is not merely a city within Italy. Since 1929, it has been an independent nation officially called the State of the Vatican City. Its ruler is the pope, who is the head of the Roman Catholic Church. Located on the west bank of the Tiber River, Vatican City covers only 109 acres (44 hectares). In 2007, it had an official population of 821.

Vatican City is the only nation in the world that can lock its gates at night. A wall surrounds Vatican City, with an opening only at Saint Peter's Square, in front of Saint Peter's Basilica. This square, which is actually round, is large enough for hundreds of thousands of people to gather to hear the pope speak.

The city has its own phone company, radio and television stations, newspapers, money, and stamps. It even has its own army, called the Swiss Guards. For centuries, Swiss men have served in the special guard unit that protects the pope. Their colorful uniforms may have been designed by Michelangelo.

For the next fifty-nine years, the pope, living in the Vatican in the heart of Rome, regarded himself as a prisoner in a foreign land. Then, in 1929, the church signed the Lateran Treaty. The treaty made Vatican City an independent state. It also made Roman Catholicism the Italian state religion and required Italian children to attend classes in religion, even in the public schools.

The church's influence on Italian law and society has waned over the years. After World War II, a new Italian constitution guaranteed freedom of religion. In 1970, the parliament passed a law allowing divorce even though the Catholic Church is opposed to divorce. In 1984, the Italian government and the Vatican signed a new agreement, making religious education a matter of choice and officially ending Roman Catholicism's position as the state religion.

Religious Holidays

Epiphany	January 6
Easter	March or April
Assumption Day	August 15
All Saints' Day	November 1
Immaculate Conception	December 8
Christmas Day	December 25
Saint Stephen's Day	December 26

The Church Today

If you ask Italians what religion they are, most of them will say Roman Catholic. In many villages, religious processions still

A band plays at a mass celebrating the feast of Saint John.

Religions of Italy

Roman Catholicism	83%
None	15%
Islam	1%
Other	1%
(Judaism, Protestantism)	

Muslims in Rome attend a mosque on the first day of 'Id al-Adha, the Feast of the Sacrifice.

wind through the streets on special occasions, such as Good Friday, which commemorates the death of Jesus.

Other Religions

Islam is Italy's second most common religion. Muslims have lived in Italy in small numbers since soon after Islam was founded in the 600s. Sicily and Sardinia were Muslim countries for five hundred years in the Middle Ages. After about 1300, Islam disappeared from Italy, but today it is returning. An increasing number of immigrants are bringing the religion back to Italy.

The first mosque, or Muslim house of worship, to be built in Italy in the modern era opened in Catania, Sicily, in 1980. In 1995, Europe's largest mosque opened in Rome. The nation of Saudi Arabia paid for its construction, which took two decades.

A small number of Italians are active in Protestant churches. Among the largest groups are Pentecostals, Assemblies of God, and Jehovah's Witnesses. Many of these groups have seen their

numbers rise as more immigrants move to Italy. But about thirty thousand Italians, mostly in the northwest, belong to the Waldensian-Methodist Church, which traces its origins back to medieval times.

Jewish people have lived in Italy since the Middle Ages, though their numbers have never been large. Today, there are about thirty thousand Jewish Italians. Venice, Florence, Rome, and other cities have synagogues, Jewish houses of worship.

On May 23, 2004, a ceremony was held at Rome's central synagogue to mark the one hundredth anniversary of its construction. Two Catholic cardinals (extreme right of photo, in red caps) joined Jewish leaders and worshippers at the gathering.

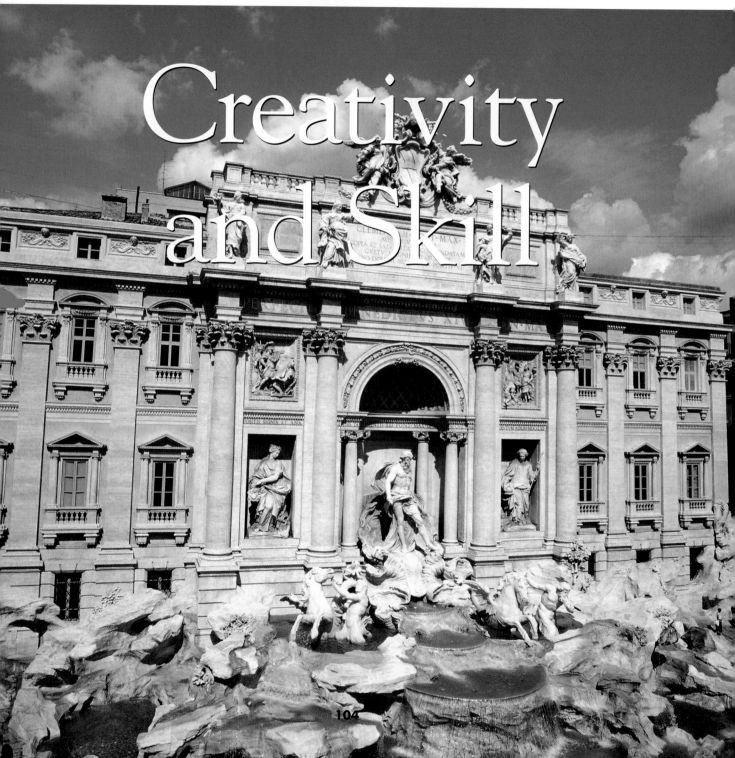

Creativity and Skill

Italy's contributions to Western culture have been great in painting, sculpture, literature, architecture, and music. The Renaissance defined several centuries for the whole of Europe. And in the twentieth century, Italian filmmakers led a new art form, the cinema.

Italy has 710 state museums, galleries, and archaeological sites. Various municipalities, the Roman Catholic Church, and private individuals own another 2,300 such sites. The art and culture of these places are not only for tourists. They are a part of every Italian's daily life.

Opposite: **The Trevi Fountain in Rome was completed in 1751. According to legend, visitors who toss a coin in the fountain will return to Rome someday.**

The Uffizi Gallery in Florence is one of the oldest art museums in the world. Its galleries contain works by artists such as Leonardo da Vinci and Michelangelo.

Italy has produced some of the most magnificent and influential art in human history. In the Middle Ages, the people in paintings looked flat and unrealistic. In the 1200s, a painter from Florence named Giotto began moving away from this. His figures look more realistic and their clothes drape

The Renaissance Man

A "Renaissance man" is a person—especially an artist—who is capable of doing great work in many different fields. Perhaps the greatest Renaissance man of all was Leonardo da Vinci. Born in Vinci, near Florence, in 1452, Leonardo became a painter, sculptor, mathematician, engineer, architect, writer, and even a festival planner. He designed a canal to connect Florence to the sea, and he cut open human corpses so that he could better understand human anatomy. In his notebooks, he sketched ideas for devices such as helicopters that were not "invented" by others until hundreds of years later.

But it is as a painter that Leonardo is best remembered. In Milan, he created *The Last Supper*. This enormous painting, 29 feet by 15 feet (9 m by 4.5 m), covers an entire wall. It shows Jesus having a final meal with his disciples, his twelve closest followers. At this meal, Jesus announces that one of them will betray him. Many other artists had painted this scene, but Leonardo's painting was remarkable because it depicted the disciples as very real human beings. Profound and subtle emotions play across their faces. Subtlety is also the hallmark of his most famous

painting—and one of the most famous paintings in the world—*Mona Lisa*. It is a portrait of a woman with a faint smile on her face. Her mysterious look fascinates viewers to this day.

more naturally. In the coming years, other painters would focus on making figures both perfectly realistic and individual. This was the beginning of the Renaissance.

The height of the Renaissance was the late 1400s and early 1500s. During this period, Leonardo da Vinci painted his massive fresco *The Last Supper* in Milan. Michelangelo carved *David*, the ideal of human beauty. Giovanni Bellini and Titian created rich, almost glowing, paintings in Venice.

Architecture also blossomed during the Renaissance. The Renaissance architects designed buildings that emphasized light, balance, and spa-

The dome on the cathedral in Florence was completed in 1436. To this day, it rises high above the city's skyline.

ciousness. One of the earliest examples of Renaissance architecture is the dome of the cathedral in Florence, designed by Filippo Brunelleschi. In the early 1500s, Donato Bramante made the plan for the new, larger Saint Peter's Basilica in Rome. Michelangelo designed the huge dome that put the finishing touch on the building.

By the late 1500s, some Italian painters were moving away from the perfect Renaissance figures. They wanted to make their own personality and feelings more central to their work. In Rome in the late 1500s and early 1600s, Caravaggio made paintings that were filled with dramatic lighting and extreme emotion.

Verdi and Politics

Giuseppe Verdi (1813–1901) composed some of the greatest operas ever written, including *La Traviata, Macbeth, Aïda, Rigoletto, A Masked Ball,* and *Il Trovatore.*

In the time leading up to Italy's unification in 1861, audiences who applauded Verdi were declaring themselves to be in favor of independence. This was because the letters in his name were said to stand for the Italian words *Vittorio Emanuele, Re di Italia,* meaning "Victor Emmanuel, King of Italy." Later, Victor Emmanuel did become king of the new Italy.

Theater and Opera

The performing arts were important to ancient Romans. They built amphitheaters in natural bowls in the earth, where the audience sat in rows of marble seats that fanned out from a small stage. Some theaters were so well designed that a person whispering in the middle of the stage could be heard perfectly in the back rows.

Several such amphitheaters are still used for productions. One of the largest is in Verona. Other ancient ruins are used as dramatic settings for opera, music, and theater. The Baths of Caracalla, in Rome, provide the stage set for productions such as the opera *Aïda* by Giuseppe Verdi.

For centuries, most dramatic plays performed in Italy were religious in nature. Then, during the Renaissance, composers started setting plays to music and using nonreligious themes. These musical plays were called operas, from the Italian phrase *opera in musica*, meaning "work in music." The performers sang their lines rather than speaking them. Even as opera became popular around the world, many composers from other countries continued to write operas in Italian.

One of the most illustrious theaters in the world is La Scala. This opera house in Milan opened in 1778, replacing an earlier theater that had burned down, and became closely associated with Verdi in the 1800s. Seriously damaged during World War II, it was rebuilt and reopened within months after the end of the war.

La Scala, which was built between 1776 and 1778, replaced a theater that had burned down.

Equally famous is Teatro La Fenice, "The Phoenix," an opera house in Venice. Like the legendary bird called the phoenix, it keeps rising from the ashes. It has been burned and rebuilt twice. The last fire, in 1996, completely destroyed the historic building. A replacement theater opened in 2003 to the joy of Venetians, tourists, and opera lovers.

Through the years, Italy has produced many world-renowned opera stars. Many opera lovers believe that the greatest singer ever was Naples-born Enrico Caruso. He began singing with the Metropolitan Opera of New York City in 1903 and was a mainstay of the company for seventeen years. He died young, at age forty-eight, of pneumonia. Luciano Pavarotti, a native of Modena, brought opera to a wider audience in the late twentieth century.

La Fenice was rebuilt from 2001 to 2003. It was designed in the style of the nineteenth century.

Popular Music

Italian popular music often has political themes. A type of music called *posse* is similar to political rap in the United States. It became popular in the late 1980s. Performers from southern Italy often use posse to express their opinions about the north's attitude toward the south.

Hip-hop reached Italy a few years later. It was made popular there by a Roman musician named Jovanotti. A Milan band called Articolo 31 soon followed; their name refers to freedom of the press. Rock, too, tends to be political. Leading Italian rock musicians include Vasco Rossi and singer-songwriter Francesco Guccini.

Literature

With a literary history starting back in Roman times, Italy has contributed greatly to world literature. Much of what we know about the story of early Rome we owe to a Roman historian named Livy (59 B.C.–A.D. 17), who wrote a massive work called *The History of Rome*. The poet Virgil told tales of Rome in his epic poem *Aeneid*.

Italy's first great writer in Tuscan Italian, rather than Latin, was Dante Alighieri. Born in 1265 in Florence, he spent many years writing a long, dramatic, rhythmic poem called *The Divine Comedy*. It tells the story of a man's journey through hell, purgatory, and paradise. *The Divine Comedy* is regarded as one of the world's great works of literature.

Dante Alighieri began work on *The Divine Comedy* in about 1307. He spent more than ten years writing it.

A Boy Made of Wood

A writer from Florence named Carlo Collodi (1826–1890) created one of the best-loved characters in all of children's literature. Pinocchio is a mischievous wooden puppet who dreams of being a real boy. A poor woodcarver named Geppetto carves the puppet and teaches him to walk. From that time on, Pinocchio is always getting into trouble. When he lies about what he has done, his nose grows longer.

Collodi used Pinocchio's adventures to teach values such as honesty, generosity, and hard work.

Writer Grazia Deledda was born in Sardinia in 1871. She explored moral conflicts and the culture of her island in her work.

Several Italian writers have won the Nobel Prize for Literature. The first Nobel Prize awarded to an Italian went to Giosuè Carducci in 1906. A professor at Bologna University, he wrote both poetry and prose. Other Italian writers to win the prize include novelist Grazia Deledda (1926), playwright Luigi Pirandello (1934), poet Salvatore Quasimodo (1959), and poet and translator Eugenio Montale (1975). In 1997, playwright Dario Fo won the award for his biting work, which often criticizes Italian society and the Catholic Church.

Film

The Italian film industry dates back to the beginning of the twentieth century. The first successful films made in Italy were about the Roman Empire. The filmmakers didn't need to build sets; they simply filmed in Rome itself. The first international film festival was held in Venice in 1932. The Venice Film Festival has been held every year since, making it the longest-running film festival in the world.

In the 1930s, Benito Mussolini forced U.S. and other foreign film companies out of Italy and established Cinecittà (Cinema City), a huge film studio that is still used today. The biggest names in the Italian film industry established themselves in the late 1940s and the 1950s. Directors such as Roberto Rossellini, Vittorio de Sica, and Federico Fellini made stars of actors such as Sophia Loren and Marcello Mastroianni.

American actor Clint Eastwood made *A Fistful of Dollars* in 1964 for Italian director Sergio Leone. The film's international success opened Italy's movie studios to a new, profitable period of making movies set in the American West but produced in Italy, called "spaghetti Westerns." More than four hundred such films were made over the next decade. Rome-born Ennio Morricone provided the music for many spaghetti Westerns.

Sports

Soccer, or football, is the most popular sport in Italy. Children play soccer in squares, on streets, and in fields. Almost every community has a soccer team, and when local teams play on Sunday afternoon, everything else stops.

The Italian League, which has existed since 1898, is regarded as one of the toughest in the world. Rivalries between towns can be bitter and raucous, and sometimes even violent. In Rome, the two main competing teams—Roma and Lazio—play their home games in the same stadium, Stadio Olimpico, which holds more than eighty-two thousand spectators.

The Italian national soccer team celebrates its World Cup victory in 2006.

Every four years, national soccer teams from around the globe compete in the World Cup, the world's biggest soccer tournament. Italy has won the World Cup four times, in 1934, 1938, 1982, and 2006, making the country's team second only to Brazil's in number of wins.

The Sporting Arena

Rome's Colosseum, which opened in A.D. 80, was built specifically for sporting competitions. About fifty thousand spectators sat on terraced marble benches that formed an oval. Below the arena were dressing rooms and holding chambers where animals were kept.

Most of the competitions held in the Colosseum involved deadly combat. Sometimes, fighters called gladiators would battle each other, and sometimes they would battle animals. In both cases, the participants fought to the death.

Today, visitors to the ruins of the Colosseum can look down on the arena and imagine the cheers of the audience, the snarls of the angry lions, and the moans of the anguished losers.

Other sports are also popular in Italy. Italians have been playing basketball for more than a century. Many American basketball players go to Italy to play on the professional teams there. Baseball and volleyball are also gaining popularity in Italy.

Italy has hosted the Olympic Games three times. The 1956 Winter Olympics were held at Cortina d'Ampezzo and nearby Zuel in the Dolomite Alps. The 1960 Summer Olympics in Rome gave Italy a chance to show the world how well it had recovered from World War II. When Turin hosted the 2006 Winter Olympics, many events took place outside the city, in the mountains nearby.

Italy won five gold medals at the Turin Olympics and took all the medals in the cross-country skiing relay. Enrico Fabris, a native of Asiago, won Italy's first-ever medal in speed skating. One of Italy's most successful Olympic athletes is downhill skier Alberto Tomba. He won gold medals in 1988 and 1992.

No matter the event, Italian sports fans are known the world over for their enthusiasm. When they're not attending an event, they're talking about it. That's half the fun!

Italian speed skater Enrico Fabris won two gold medals and one bronze medal in the Winter Olympic Games in Turin in 2006.

The Best of Life

A family in Palermo enjoys an outdoor meal.

I T HAS BEEN SAID THAT ITALY OFFERS THE BEST OF EVERY-thing in life. Certainly, many Italians think so. Italians are serious about their endeavors, but most try to have fun whatever they do.

Family Life

Family is everything to Italians. Children grow up surrounded by members of their extended family—parents, grandparents, aunts, and uncles. Each adult does whatever needs to be done to keep each nearby child safe and happy.

Opposite: **Local cheeses are displayed in Sassari, Sardinia. Cheese is an important element of Italian cuisine.**

Many grandparents help out with child care. This grandfather is taking a child to school.

But the structure of the Italian family is changing. About half of Italian men live at home with their parents at age thirty. Many are unable to find good jobs that would allow them to live on their own. At the same time, many Italian women now work. Grandparents are often enlisted to take care of children. Daycare centers are also becoming more popular, especially in cities.

Traditionally, Italians had big families. But in recent years, the number of children in the average family has dropped drastically. Italy's birthrate is now among the lowest in the world. In 2007, Italian women were having an average of only 1.29 children. In 1971, the rate was 3.4 children per woman.

The government is hunting for ways to encourage women to have more children. It offers child-care benefits and payments to new mothers.

Small families may mean that in the future fewer people will pay into the pension system that most Italians rely on to support them in their old age. Italy now has the oldest population in Europe—20 percent of all Italians are older than sixty-five. If this trend continues, only immigration will keep the age distribution of Italy's population in balance.

Men gather at a café. The average Italian man lives to be seventy-seven years old.

Education

Children in Italy must go to school from age six until age fourteen. Primary school goes through age eleven, when children move to lower secondary school (like middle school in North America). About 80 percent of children continue their education through high school or go to a technical institute.

Students who go to college usually attend one in their own city and live at home. Few universities have housing for students.

Elementary school students at their desks in a classroom in Asolo in northern Italy

University education in Italy began in ancient times. A school of medicine was founded in Salerno in the ninth century. The University of Bologna, founded in the eleventh century, is probably the oldest full university in Europe. It has about one hundred thousand students.

The University of Rome was founded by the Catholic Church in about 1300 and remained primarily a religious institution for hundreds of years. When Rome became part of modern Italy, the university became a state university. Often called La Sapienza, meaning "Knowledge," it is Europe's largest university, with nearly 150,000 students.

Students study in a library reading hall at the University of Pavia, one of the oldest universities in Europe.

Pesto

The vivid green pasta sauce called pesto originated in Genoa. Today, it is one of the most popular pasta sauces. Have an adult help you make this simple recipe with a food processor.

Ingredients

2 cups fresh basil leaves, packed

$\frac{1}{3}$ cup pine nuts

3 medium garlic cloves, minced

$\frac{1}{2}$ cup olive oil

$\frac{1}{2}$ cup freshly grated Parmesan cheese

salt and pepper to taste

Directions

Put the basil and the pine nuts in a food processor and chop. Add the garlic and process until the mixture is chopped finely. With the food processor on, slowly add the olive oil in a constant stream. Add the cheese and mix until blended. Add salt and pepper to taste. Serve over pasta. This recipe makes about 1 cup.

Glorious Food

Italians are known the world over for their food. Each region of Italy enjoys its own kind of cooking. For example, in Naples, pasta is served with a tomato-based sauce, while in the north, it is more often served with a white cheese sauce. The people of Genoa often put pesto, a flavorful mixture of basil, pine nuts, garlic, olive oil, and grated cheese, on their pasta.

The grated cheese called Parmesan originated in the area around Parma. Italians also invented many other cheeses, including Gorgonzola, mozzarella, provolone, and ricotta.

No one knows when pizza was invented, but the people of Naples made it popular. At first, pizza was a simple flatbread topped with tomato and garlic. Since then, it has evolved into countless variations, served all over Italy and the world.

Italians tend to eat a light breakfast of coffee and perhaps a small bun. Lunch is often the main meal, while dinner tends to be lighter. Italian meals may include antipasti, an array of

Italian pizza often has thinner crust than pizza in North America, and the edges are sometimes burned.

vegetables, cold cuts, and seafood; a pasta dish; a main course of meat or fish; a salad; and cheese and fruit. Bread is served with every meal.

Italy is justly famous for its ice cream, which is called *gelato*. Fresh gelato is made regularly at ice cream shops called *gelaterias*. Italians are just as likely to gather, discussing sports and the world, in a gelateria as in a coffee shop.

Gelato comes in hundreds of different flavors. Chocolate, fruits, and nuts are common ingredients.

Many Italians drink a strong, dark coffee called espresso, which is served in tiny cups. Another type of Italian coffee, cappuccino, is espresso mixed with hot, frothed milk. Both espresso and cappuccino have become popular in North America. Meanwhile, many Italians are becoming increasingly fond of American-style fast food, a trend that bothers some Italians.

In general, dinner is served later at night in southern Italy than in northern Italy. This is because many people in the south, as in most Mediterranean regions, traditionally took naps in the afternoon during the hottest part of the day. These naps are rapidly disappearing as a regular part of life, although many businesses still shut down for several hours in the early afternoon.

The first coffeehouse in Europe opened in Venice in the seventeenth century. Coffee remains central to Italian life.

Celebrations

Christmas is Italy's biggest holiday. Stores decorate in gold, silver, red, and white. At home, many people celebrate Christmas Eve with a huge feast, often featuring fish. The Christmas season in Italy lasts until Epiphany, January 6, the date when the Three Wise Men are said to have reached Jesus's manger.

National Holidays in Italy	
New Year's Day	January 1
Liberation Day	April 25
Labor Day	May 1
Anniversary of the Republic	June 2
National Unity Day	November 5

Befana puppets are sold in a square in Rome before Christmas.

Santa Claus, or Saint Nicholas, is mainly a northern European traditional figure, but one that Italians now often celebrate. Traditionally, Italian children become excited about a different gift-giving figure—Befana, whose name comes from the Italian word for Epiphany, *Epifania*. Befana was supposedly a woman who meant to go with the Wise Men but was too busy. She planned to see them on their way back, but they returned by a different route. Since then, each year on Epiphany, she busily searches for them, riding on a broomstick and bringing gifts. Children dress in costumes like Befana and go to neighboring houses, where they receive small gifts such as fruit and nuts. At the end of the Befana celebration, Befana figures are burned in a bonfire to get rid of the old year and start the new year afresh.

Another major festival is Carnevale. It is a huge festival celebrated in the last week before Lent, a serious forty-day period that precedes Easter. Italy's biggest Carnevale celebration is in Venice, where people dress in dazzling costumes and parade around the city. Though the costumes often feature somber masks, Carnevale is a time for giddy fun. Children run about throwing confetti. Shopkeepers pass out snacks in the city's squares. Music fills the air. Like Italy itself, it is a feast for the senses.

Carnevale costumes in Venice generally include masks. The costumes feature rich colors and exquisite detail.

Timeline

Italy History

Ancient people make petroglyphs in Val Camonica.	8000 B.C.
Etruscans develop a powerful civilization.	800s B.C.
Greeks begin building the city of Syracuse on Sicily.	734 B.C.
The Roman Republic is established.	509 B.C.
Hannibal leads Carthaginian troops across the Alps.	218 B.C.–217 B.C.
Rome destroys Carthage.	146 B.C.
Julius Caesar gains power in Rome.	49 B.C.
Julius Caesar is murdered; the Roman Republic ends.	44 B.C.
Augustus Caesar becomes the first Roman emperor.	27 B.C.
Constantine moves the capital of the Roman Empire to Constantinople.	A.D. 324
The Visigoths sack Rome.	410
The Huns invade Rome.	452
The Ostrogoths invade Italy.	488
The Lombards control much of Italy.	564–774
The Normans conquer Sicily.	1060
The Renaissance begins in Italy.	1300s

World History

2500 B.C.	Egyptians build the pyramids and the Sphinx in Giza.
563 B.C.	The Buddha is born in India.
A.D. 313	The Roman emperor Constantine legalizes Christianity.
610	The Prophet Muhammad begins preaching a new religion called Islam.
1054	The Eastern (Orthodox) and Western (Roman Catholic) Churches break apart.
1095	The Crusades begin.
1215	King John seals the Magna Carta.
1300s	The Renaissance begins in Italy.
1347	The plague sweeps through Europe.
1453	Ottoman Turks capture Constantinople, conquering the Byzantine Empire.
1492	Columbus arrives in North America.

Italy History

Rulers from Spain, Austria, and France vie for control of Italy.	**1500s–early 1800s**
The Kingdom of Italy is established under King Victor Emmanuel II.	**1861**
Benito Mussolini takes control of Italy.	**1922**
Vatican City becomes an independent state.	**1929**
Italy colonizes Ethiopia.	**1936**
Mussolini forms an alliance with Germany.	**1940**
Allied troops land in Italy.	**1943**
The Republic of Italy is established.	**1946**
Italy's constitution goes into effect.	**1948**
Italy is struck by terrorist bombings.	**Late 1960–1970s**
Many leading politicians are arrested in an anticorruption program.	**Early 1990s**
Italy begins to use the euro, the European Union's common currency.	**2002**
Election laws are revised to help stabilize the government	**2005**
Italy defeats France to win soccer's World Cup.	**2006**

World History

1500s	Reformers break away from the Catholic Church, and Protestantism is born.
1776	The U.S. Declaration of Independence is signed.
1789	The French Revolution begins.
1865	The American Civil War ends.
1879	The first practical light bulb is invented.
1914	World War I begins.
1917	The Bolshevik Revolution brings communism to Russia.
1929	A worldwide economic depression begins.
1939	World War II begins.
1945	World War II ends.
1957	The Vietnam War begins.
1969	Humans land on the Moon.
1975	The Vietnam War ends.
1989	The Berlin Wall is torn down as communism crumbles in Eastern Europe.
1991	The Soviet Union breaks into separate countries.
2001	Terrorists attack the World Trade Center in New York City and the Pentagon in Arlington, Virginia.

Fast Facts

Official name: Repubblica Italiana (Republic of Italy)

Capital: Rome

Official language: Italian

Rome

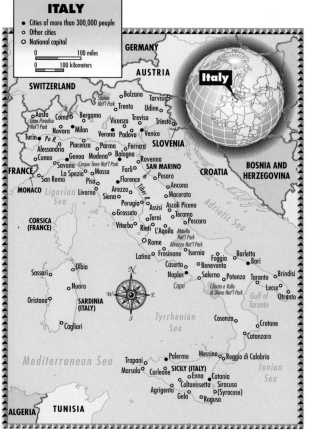

Italy's flag

Apennines

Year of founding:	1861, Kingdom of Italy 1946, Republic of Italy
National anthem:	"Il Conti degli Italiani" ("The Song of the Italians")
Government:	Republic
Chief of state:	President
Head of government:	Prime minister
Area:	116,313 square miles (301,249 sq km)
Greatest distance north and south:	760 miles (1,220 km)
Greatest distance east and west:	320 miles (515 km)
Latitude and longitude of geographic center:	42°50' N, 12°50' E
Bordering countries:	France to the northwest, Switzerland and Austria to the north, and Slovenia to the northeast
Highest elevation:	Monte Bianco (Mont Blanc), 15,771 feet (4,807 m) above sea level
Lowest elevation:	Sea level along the coasts
Average high temperatures:	Rome: 52°F (11°C) in January, 86°F (30°C) in July; Milan: 41°F (5°C) in January, 84°F (29°C) in July
Average precipitation extremes:	31 inches (79 cm) in Rome; 38 inches (97 cm) in Milan

Saint Peter's Basilica

**National population
(2007 est.):** 58,147,733

**Population of largest
cities (2007 est.):**

Rome	2,648,000
Milan	1,305,000
Naples	1,047,000
Turin	921,000
Palermo	689,000
Genoa	656,000

Famous landmarks:
- ▶ *Basilica of San Marco,* Venice
- ▶ *Colosseum,* Rome
- ▶ *La Scala,* Milan
- ▶ *Mount Etna,* Sicily
- ▶ *Pompeii,* near Naples
- ▶ *Saint Peter's Basilica,* Vatican City

Industry: Tourism is Italy's biggest industry. Service industries such as trade, restaurants, hotels, banking, and real estate provide 63 percent of Italy's national income, and manufacturing industries provide about 25 percent. Major manufactured goods include steel, automobiles, machinery, food products, wine, and clothing. Italy's most valuable mineral product is natural gas. Salt, feldspar, talc, lignite, coal, and lead are also mined. Major agricultural products include olives, grapes, wheat, and sugar beets.

Currency: The euro; in 2008, US$1.00 equaled about 0.63 euros, and 1.00 euro equaled US$1.58.

**Weights and
measures:** The metric system

Literacy rate: 98.4%

Currency

Schoolgirl

Giuseppe Verdi

Common Italian words and phrases:

buon giorno	hello; good day
buona sera	good evening
ciao!	hi! (or bye!)
arrivederci	good-bye
per favore	please
grazie	thank you
Come ti chiani?	What is your name?
Dov'è . . . ?	Where is . . . ?
scusi	excuse me; sorry

Famous Italians:

Dante Alighieri (1265–1321)
Poet

Giorgio Armani (1934–)
Fashion designer

Michelangelo Buonarroti (1475–1564)
Painter and sculptor

Galileo Galilei (1564–1642)
Scientist

Sophia Loren (1934–)
Actor

Benito Mussolini (1883–1945)
Dictator

Marco Polo (1254–1324)
Traveler and writer

Miuccia Prada (1949–)
Fashion designer

Roberto Rossellini (1906–1977)
Film director

Giuseppe Verdi (1813–1901)
Opera composer

Leonardo da Vinci (1452–1519)
Painter and inventor

To Find Out More

Books

▶ Adkins, Lesley, and Roy A. Adkins. *Handbook to Life in Ancient Rome*. New York: Facts on File, 2004.

▶ Anderson, Robert. *Italy*. Washington, DC: National Geographic, 2006.

▶ Blanch, Gregory, and Roberta Stathis. *Renaissance Artists Who Inspired the World*. Brea, CA: Ballard & Tighe, 2003.

▶ Deckker, Zilah. *National Geographic Investigates Ancient Rome: Archaeology Unlocks the Secrets of Rome's Past*. Washington, DC: National Geographic, 2007.

▶ Lace, William W. *The Vatican*. Lucent Books, 2005.

▶ Lusted, Marcia. *The Canals of Venice*. Lucent Books, 2003.

▶ Nesbitt, Mark R. *Living in Renaissance Italy*. Detroit: Greenhaven Press, 2005.

▶ Winter, Jane Kohen, and Leslie Jermyn. *Italy*. New York: Benchmark Books, 2003.

DVDs

▶ *Discovery Atlas: Italy Revealed*. Image Entertainment, 2007.

▶ *Florence: Birthplace of the Renaissance*. Educational Video Network, 2004.

▶ *Mussolini: Italy's Nightmare*. A&E Home Video, 2005.

▶ *Vatican City: Art & Glory*. V.I.E.W., Inc., 2007.

▶ *Venice: Tides of Change*. CustomFlix, 2007.

▶ *Visions of Italy*. Acorn Media, 2005.

Web Sites

▶ **The Italian Government Tourist Board**
www.italiantourism.com
For lots of information on where to go and what to do in Italy.

▶ **Italy Guides**
www.italyguides.it
Go sightseeing on your computer with visits to Rome, Venice, Florence, Pisa, Siena, Naples, and more.

▶ **Made in Italy On Line**
www.made-in-italy.com
To view Italian products such as fashion, automobiles, food, and wine.

▶ **U.S. Department of State: Background Note—Italy**
www.state.gov/r/pa/ei/bgn/4033.htm
A site that covers Italy's geography, people, and government and is updated regularly.

▶ **Vinci: Leonardo's Home Town**
www.leonet.it/comuni/vinci/
To learn more about Leonardo da Vinci and see the town where he grew up.

Embassies and Organizations

▶ **Embassy of Italy**
3000 Whitehaven St., NW
Washington, DC 20008
202-612-4400
www.ambwashingtondc.esteri.it

▶ **Embassy of Italy in Canada**
275 Slater Street, 21st Floor
Ottawa, Ontario K1P 5H9
Canada
613-232-2401
www.ambottawa.esteri.it/
ambasciata_ottawa

Index

Page numbers in *italics* indicate illustrations.

A

Abruzzi region, 18
Abruzzo National Park, 38, *38*, *39*
A.C. Milan (soccer team), 63
Adriatic Sea, 15, 18, 20, 80
Aeolian Islands, 24
African colonies, 58, 59
agriculture, 31, 41, 78–80
Agrigento, 12, *12*
Aïda (Giuseppe Verdi), 11, 108
Alfonso V (Aragonian king), 51
Alighieri, Dante, 111, *111*, 133
Allied powers, 60, 61
Alps mountain range, 16, 17, 18, 25, 33, 34, 46
Altagnana, *15*
Alto Adige region, 59
Amalfi, 19
Amalfi Drive, 19
amphitheaters, 108
anarchists, 62
animal life
    birds, 35, *35*, 39
    brown bears, 32, *32*, 39
    chamois, 34, *34*, 37, 39
    at Colosseum, 96, 114
    conservation, *32*, 33
    endangered species, 32, 38, 39
    foxes, 34, 39
    horses, 9, *9*, 46
    ibexes, 34, *34*, 37
    livestock, 31, 41, 79–80
    Rocco (truffle dog), 30
    rodents, 34
    wolves, 32–33, *33*, 38–39
antipasti (foods), 123–124
Antony, Mark, 47, *47*
Apennines mountain range, 16, 18, 19, 23, 33, 38
Appian Way, 45
Arab people, 50, 51, 58
architecture, 105, 107, *107*
Arco, *40*
Armani, Giorgio, 82, *82*, 133
art, 13, 21, 25, *25*, 27, 43, 54, 55, *55*, 75, 84, 97, *97*, 105, *105*
Articolo 31 (musical group), 111
artifacts, *40*
Asolo, *120*
Assisi, 25, *25*
A/X (Armani Exchange), 82
Axis powers, 60

B

Basilica of Saint Francis of Assisi, 25
Basilica of San Marco, 52, *52*
basketball, 115
Baths of Caracalla, 108
Battle of Actium, 47
Bay of Naples, 23
Befana celebrations, 126, *126*
Bellini, Giovanni, 107
Beretta firearms, 82
Berlusconi, Silvio, 63, *63*, 70
birds, 35, *35*, 39
Blue Grotto (sea cave), 23
Bologna, 62
Bonaparte, Joseph, 56
Bonaparte, Napoléon, 55, 56, *56*
Borgia family, 54
Botticelli, Sandro, 84
Bramante, Donato, 107
Brunelleschi, Filippo, 107

C

Cabrini, Maria Francesca, 92, *92*
Caesar, Augustus, 47, *47*
Caesar, Julius, 46–47
Capitoline, 74–75
cappuccino (coffee), 125, *125*
Capri, 12, 23
Caravaggio (artist), 107
Carboneria (secret society), 56
Carducci, Giosuè, 112
Carnevale celebration, 127, *127*
Caruso, Enrico, 110
Castel del Monte, 84
catacombs, 96, *96*
Catania, 102
cave paintings, 21
caves, 12, 21, 23
Cavour, Camillo Benso di, 57
Chamber of Deputies, 65, 67, 71
Charlemagne (Frankish leader), 50, *50*
cheeses, 80, 117, 123
Christian Democratic Party, 62, 63
Christianity, 48, 95–97, 102–103.
    See also Roman Catholic Church.
Cimabue (artist), 25
Cinecittà (Cinema City), 112
Cinque Terre ("Five Lands"), 21, *21*
cities. *See also* communes; towns.
    Agrigento, 12, *12*
    Bologna, 62
    Catania, 102
    Constantinople, 48, *48*, 50, 96
    Florence, 54, *77*, 86, 103, *105*, 107, *107*

Genoa, 52, 82, 83, 87, 122
Herculaneum, 24
Magna Graecia cluster, 43
Maranello, 83
Milan, 11, *11*, 27, 49, 61, 69, 69,
    82, 87, 107, 109
Naples, 27, 49, 51, 56, 57, 87,
    122, 123
Paestum, 43
Palermo, 21, 50, 87, 88, *117*
Perugia, 49
Pompeii, 24, *24*
Populonia, *42*
Poseidonia, 43
Rome, 11, 26, 33, 44–45, 47, 48,
    49, 53, 54, 56, *72*, 74–75, *74*,
    75, 78, 87, 90, 96, 97, 98, 99,
    100, 102, *104*, 107, 108, 111,
    113, 114
Sarno, 30
Siena, 8, 9
Syracuse, 43
Turin, 27, 82, 83, 87
Udine, 26
Vatican City, *94*, 100, *100*
Venice, 20, *20*, 49, 51, 52, 53, 55,
    56, *60*, *76*, 78, 103, 107, 110
civil war, 47, 61
Cleopatra (Egyptian ruler), 47, *47*
climate, 25–26, *26*, 30, 31, 125
Collodi, Carlo, 111
Colosseum, 114, *114*
Columbus, Christopher, 53, *53*, 91
communes. *See also* cities, towns.
    government of, 73
    Malcesine, *17*
communism, 59, 62
Communist Party, 62
Constantine (emperor), 48, *48*, 96
Constantinople, 48, *48*, 50, 96

Constitutional Court, 69
Corno Grande peak, 18, *18*
Cortina d'Ampezzo, 115
Council of Ministers, 68
currency (euro), 84, *84*, 85
currency (lira), 84

D
Dante (author), 93
David (Michaelangelo), 55, 107
Deledda, Grazia, 112, *112*
Diocletian (emperor), 48
The Divine Comedy
    (Dante Alighieri), 111
Dolomite mountains, 17
Ducati motorcycles, 84

E
Eastern Orthodox Church.
    See Orthodox Church.
Eastwood, Clint, 113
economy
    agriculture, 78–80
    automobile manufacturing, 83, *83*
    family-owned businesses, 81
    fashion design, 82, *82*
    foreign competition, 81–82
    government and, 85
    imports, 81
    manufacturing, 62, 80–84, *81*,
        83, 83
    mining, 23, 80
    publishing industry, 82
    size of, 63, 77
    stock exchange, 82
    tourism, 12, 17, *76*, 77–78, *77*,
        78, 86
    "value-added" work, 81
espresso (coffee), 125
Ethiopia, 58, 59–60

Etruria (Etruscan homeland), 42
Etruscan people, 42–43, *42*, 44
euro (currency), 84, *84*, 85
European Union (EU), 84, 85, *85*
executive branch of government,
    64, 66, 67–68, *67*

F
Fabris, Enrico, 115, *115*
Famous people, 133, *133*
fascists, 59, 60, 62
fashion design, 11, *11*, 82, *82*
fast food, 125
Fellini, Federico, 112
Ferrari automobiles, 83, *83*
Fiat automobiles, 27, 83
film industry, 112–113
flooding, 20
Florence, 54, *77*, 86, 103, *105*,
    107, *107*
Fontana, Domenico, 24
foods, 79, *117*, 122–124, *122*, 125
Forum, 75, *75*
Forza Party, *70*
four-lined snakes, 36
Franciscans, 97
Francis of Assisi, 97, *97*
Frankish people, 50
fresco paintings, 25, *25*, 107
Friulian dialect, 93

G
Galilei, Galileo, 54, *54*, 133
Gardone Val Trompia, 82
Garibaldi, Giuseppe, 57, *57*
Gasperi, Alcide de, 62
gelaterias (ice cream shop), 124, *124*
gelato (ice cream), 124, *124*
Genoa, 52, 82, 83, 87, 122

geography
    Abruzzi region, 18
    borders, 15
    caves, 12, 21, 23
    coastline, *14*, 16, 19, 23, 42, 51
    earthquakes, 25
    elevation, 16, 17, 21, 22, *37*
    glaciers, 12, 37
    islands, 12, 15, 16, 19, 20, *20*, 21,
        22–23, 24, 43, 49, 51, 52, 56,
        60, 76, 78, 107, 110
    lakes, 16, 17, *17*, 42
    mountains, 12, 16–18, *18*, 19, 22,
        23–25, 30, 31, 32, 35, *37*, 38,
        38, 39, 42, 45
    North Italian Plain, 18
    Piedmont region, 18, 30
    rivers, 16, 18, 33, 39, 42, 44,
        74, 100
    volcanoes, 16, 21–22, 23–24, *23*
Giotto (artist), 25, 106–107
glaciers, 12, 37
gladiators, 114
golden eagles, 35, *35*, 39
gondoliers, 76
government
    birthrate and, 119
    caesars, 47
    Chamber of Deputies, 65, 67, 71
    coalition parties, 71
    communism, 59, 62
    constitution, 65, 69
    Constitutional Court, 69
    consuls, 44
    as constitutional monarchy, 57
    corruption in, 63, 72, 73
    Council of Ministers, 68
    courts of appeals, 69
    courts of assizes, 69
    dictatorships, 47, 57, 59, *59*, 60,
        60, 61, 103, 112

district courts, 68
economy and, 85
elections, 66, 67, 68, *72*
emperors, 46–47
European Union (EU), 84, 85, *85*
executive branch, *64*, 66, 67–68,
    67
fascism, 59, 60, 62
judicial branch, 66, 68–69, 69
justices of the peace, 68
legislative branch, 65–66, *65*, 67
local governments, 73
parliament, 57, 63, 65, 67, 68, 70,
    71, *72*, 73
political parties, 62, 67, 69–72,
    70, *71*
prime ministers, 62, 63, *63*, 67–68,
    68, 71
proportional representation, 70
religion and, 100–101
republics, 44
salaries, 73
Senate, 44, 65, 66
Supreme Court of Cassation, 69
tribunals, 69
tribunes, 44
votes of confidence, 67–68, 68
Gran Paradiso National Park, 37, *37*
Greek Empire, 12, 27, 43, 44, 93
Grillo, Beppe, 73, *73*
Guccini, Francesco, 111
Gulf of Naples, 24
Gulf of Taranto, 15

H

Hannibal (general), 46
Herculaneum, 24
historical maps. *See also* maps.
    Italian City-States (1500), *51*
    Italian Colonies in Africa
        (1937), *58*

People of Italy (500 B.C.), *43*
Roman Empire, *44*
Hitler, Adolf, 60, *60*, 61
holidays, 101–102, *101*, *102*,
    125–126, *126*
Holy Roman Empire, 50, *50*

I

'Id al-Adha (Feast of the
    Sacrifice), *102*
Immigrant Party, *71*
Ionian Sea, 15
Islamic religion, 102, *102*
islands
Aeolian Islands, 24
    Capri, 12
    Lampedusa, 89
    Sardinia, 15, 22–23, *22*, 51, 56, 102
    Sicily, 12, 15, 16, 21, 22, 24,
        25, 26, 43, 50–51, 57, *61*, 63,
        79, 102
    Venice, 20, *20*, 49, 51, 52, 53, 55,
        56, 60, 76, 78, 107, 110, 112
Italian Guard of Honor, 60
Italian Lake District, 17
Italian language, 93
Italian League, 113
Italian Riviera, 17, 19, 21, 78
Italic people, 41, 43

J

Jovanotti (musician), 111
Judaism, 60, 96, 103, *103*
judicial branch of government,
    66, 68–69, 69
Julius II (pope), 55

K

Kingdom of the Two Sicilies, 51
Kublai Khan (Mongol leader), 52

L

Lake Como, 17
Lake Garda, 16, 17, *17*
Lake Maggiore, 17
Lambretta scooters, 84
Lampedusa, 89
languages
  dialects, 93
  Etruscan, 42
  Italian, 93
  Latin, 45
La Scala theater, 109, *109*
The Last Supper (Leonardo da
  Vinci), 106
Lateran Treaty, 100
Latin language, 45
Latin people, 44
Lazio (soccer team), 113
legislative branch of government,
  65–66, *65*, 67
Leone, Sergio, 113
Ligurian Sea, 15, 17
Liguria region, *14*
lira (currency), 84
literature, 93, 111–112, *112*
livestock, 31, 41, 79–80
Livy (historian), 111
local governments, 73
Lombard tribe, 49
Lombardy region, 49, 69
Loren, Sophia, 112, 133
Lötschberg Base Tunnel, 18

M

Magna Graecia city cluster, 43
Majella National Park, 38–39
Malcesine, *17*
Mameli, Goffredo, 70
Mansouri, Mustapha, *71*
manufacturing, 62, 80–84, *81*, 83, 83

maps. *See also* historical maps.
  geopolitical, *10*
  population density, 88
  resources, *79*
  Rome, *75*
  topographical, *16*
maquis (plant), 22
Maranello, 83
Marinus (stonecutter), 19
Mark (saint), 52
Mastroianni, Marcello, 112
Medici family, 54, 55
Medici, Lorenzo de, 55
Mediterranean Sea, 12, 15, 21, 26,
  42, 44, 45, 50, 58
Michelangelo (artist), 55, 75, 100,
  105, 107, 133
Middle Ages, 53, 102, 103, 106
Milan, 11, *11*, 27, 49, 69, 69, 82, 87,
  106, 107, 109
mining, 23, 80
Missionary Sisters of the Sacred
  Heart, 92
Molinari, Anna, 11
Mona Lisa (Leonardo da Vinci),
  106, *106*
Montale, Eugenio, 112
Mont Blanc Tunnel, 18
Monte Bianco, 17
Moro, Aldo, 62
Morricone, Ennio, 113
Mount Etna, 16, 21–22, 24
Mount La Marmora, 22
Mount Stromboli, 24
Mount Vesuvius, 23–24, *23*
Mount Vulcano, 24
movies. *See* film industry.
museums, 27, 105, *105*
music, 11, 108, 109, 110–111, 113
Mussolini, Benito, 59, *59*, 60, 60, 61,
  112, 133

N

Naples, 27, 49, 51, 56, 57, 87,
  122, 123
national animal, 33
national anthem, 70
national flag, 69, 69
national holidays, 125
national parks, 37–39, *37*, 38
neofascists, 62
Norman people, 51
North Italian Plain, 18
Novaro, Michele, 70
Nuraghi people, 22, *22*
nuraghi ruins, 22, *22*

O

Olympic Games, 12, 27, 115, *115*
operas, 11, 108, 109, 110, *110*
Operation Clean Hands, 63, 72
organized crime, 63
Orthodox Church, 96–97
Ostrogoth tribe, 49, *49*
outdoor cafés, 86

P

Paestum, 43
Palatine Hill, 74
Palermo, 21, 50, 87, 88, *117*
Palio races, 9, *9*
Papal States, 49, 56, 99, *99*
parliament, 57, 63, 65, 67, 68, 70,
  71, 72, 73
Parma, 123
Parmesan cheese, 123
Pavarotti, Luciano, 110
people
  Arab, 50, 51, 58
  birthrate, 118–119
  clothing, 11, *11*, 81, 82, 82,
    87, 100

education, 100, 120–121, *120, 121*
emigrants, 58, 91, *91*, 92
employment, 84, 118
Etruscans, 42–43, *42*, 44
families, 117–119, *117, 118*
foods, 79, *117*, 122–124, *122, 123, 124*, 125
Franks, 50
immigrants, 89–90, *89, 90, 91*, 102, 103, 119
Italic, 41, 43
languages, 42, 43, 45, 93
Latins, 44
life expectancy, *119*
Lombard tribe, 49
names, 93
naps, 125
Normans, 27, 51
Nuraghi, 22, *22*
Ostrogoth tribe, 49, *49*
pension system, 119
population, 74, 87, 88, *88*, 100
prehistoric, 41
slavery, 43, 46, 57
Visigoth tribe, 49
women, 43, 61, 118–119
Perrotta, Simone, *113*
Perugia, *49*
pesto (pasta sauce), 122, *122*
Peter (disciple), 95
petroglyphs, 41, *41*
Piazza del Campo, 8, *9*
Piedmont region, 18, 30
Pinocchio (Carlo Collodi), 111
Pirandello, Luigi, 112
Pisa, Rustichello da, 52
Pistoia, *59*
Pius IX (pope), 99

pizza, 79, 80, 123, *123*
plant life, 22, 29–31, *29, 30, 31*
Polo, Marco, 52, *52*, 133
Pompeii, 24, *24*
Populonia, *42*
Po River, 16, 18
Poseidonia, 43
posse music, 110
Po Valley, 80
Prada, Miuccia, 133
Prodi, Romano, 68, 71
Protestants, 102–103
Puez-Geisler Nature Park, *28*
Punic Wars, 45, 46, *46*

Q

Quasimodo, Salvatore, 112
Quirinale Palace, 64, 67

R

railroads, 18, 21, *62*
Raphael (artist), 84
recipe, 122, *122*
Red Brigades, 62
religion
    catacombs, 96, *96*
    Christianity, 48, 95–97, 102–103
    education and, 100, 121
    Franciscans, 97
    government and, 100–101
    holidays, 101–102, *101, 102*, 125–126, *126*
    Holy Roman Empire, 50
    Islamic, 102, *102*
    Judaism, 60, 96, 103, *103*
    Lateran Treaty, 100

mosques, 102
Papal States, 49, 56, 99, *99*
popes, 49, 50, 55, 64, 92, 97–98, 99, *99*, 100
Protestants, 102–103
Roman Catholic Church, 49, 54, 92, 94, 95, *95*, 97–98, 99–101, *103*, 121
Saint Peter's Basilica, *94*, 95, *95*, 100, 107
theater and, 109
Remus (Roman hero), 33
Renaissance, 53–55, 75, 84, 93, 105, 106–107, 109
"Renaissance man," 106
reptilian life, 36, *36*
Risorgimento movement, 57
roadways, 18, 19, 42, 45
Rocco (truffle dog), 30
Roger II (Norman king), 51
Roman Catholic Church, 49, 54, 92, 94, 95, *95*, 97–98, *103*, 121. *See also* Christianity.
Roman Empire, 24, 44–46, *46–47*, 48–49, 50, *50*, 51, 58, 95, 96, 112
Roma (soccer team), 113, *113*
Rome, 11, 26, 33, 44–45, 47, 48, 49, 53, 54, 56, *72*, 74–75, *74, 75*, 78, 87, 90, 96, 97, 98, 99, 100, 102, *104*, 107, 108, 111, 113, 114
Romulus (Roman hero), 33
Rossellini, Roberto, 112, 133
Rossi, Vasco, 111
Rubens, Peter Paul, 48
ruins, 11, *12*, 22, 43, 74, 78, 108, 114, *114*

S

Saint Gotthard Pass, 18
Saint Peter's Basilica, *94*, 95, *95*, 100, 107
Saint Peter's Square, 100
Salerno, 121
San Giovanni Cathedral, 98
San Lorenzo, *87*
San Marino, 19, *19*
Santa Maria delle Grazie monastery, 27
Santa María (ship), *53*
Sardinia, 15, 22–23, *22*, 51, 56, 57, 102
Sarno, 30
Scipio Africanus (general), 46
scooters, *13*, 83–84
Second Punic War, 46, *46*
Senate, 44, *65*, 66
Seven Hills of Rome, 74–75
shipbuilding industry, 82
Shroud of Turin, 98, *98*
Sica, Vittorio de, 112
Sicily, 12, 15, 16, 21, 22, 24, 25, 26, 33, 43, 50–51, 57, *61*, 63, 79, 102
Siena, 8, *9*
Sistine Chapel, 55, *55*
skiing, 11–12
slavery, 43, 46, 57
snakes, 36, *36*
soccer, 113–114, *113*
Sorrento Peninsula, 23
"spaghetti Westerns," 113
Spartacus (slave), 46
sports, 9, *9*, 11–12, 63, 113–115
Spring Fashion Week, 11, *11*
Stadio Olimpico, 113

Strait of Messina, 21, 57
Supreme Court of Cassation, 69
Swiss Guards, 100
Syracuse, 43

T

Taurini tribe, 27
Teatro La Fenice opera house, 110, *110*
terrorism, 62, *62*
theater, 108, 109, *109*
Tiber River, 33, 44, 74, 100
Titian (artist), 107
Tomba, Alberto, 115
tourism, 12, 17, 63, *76*, 77–78, *77*, *78*, 86
towns. *See also* cities; communes.
    Altagnana, 15
    Amalfi, 19
    Cinque Terre, 21, *21*
    Cortina d'Ampezzo, 115
    Zuel, 115
transportation, *13*, 18, 83–84, *83*
trees, 29–31, *31*, 79,
Trentino region, 59
Trevi Fountain, *104*
truffles, 30, *30*
Turin, 27, 82, 83, 87
Tuscany region, *15*, 49, 78, 79, 93
Tyrrhenian Sea, 15, 19

U

Udine, 26
Uffizi Gallery, *105*
United States, 58, 60, 67, 91, *91*, 92, 125
University of Bologna, 121

University of Pavia, *121*
University of Rome, 121

V

Val Camonica region, 41, *41*
Vatican City, *94*, 100, *100*
Venice, 20, *20*, 49, 51, 52, 53, 55, 56, *60*, 76, 78, 103, 107, 110
Venice Film Festival, 112
Verdi, Giuseppe, 11, 108, *108*, 109, 133, *133*
Verona, 108
Vespa scooters, 83–84
Victor Emmanuel II (king), 57, 108
Vinci, Leonardo da, 27, 84, *105*, 106, 107, 133
Virgil (poet), 111
Visigoth tribe, 49
volcanoes, 16, 21–22, 23–24, *23*

W

Waldensian-Methodist Church, 103
wildlife. *See* animal life; plant life; reptilian life.
winemaking, 27, 79
Winter Olympics, 12
women, 43, 61, 118–119
World Cup soccer tournament, *113*, 114
World War I, 59
World War II, 60–61, *61*, 96, 109, 115

Z

Zuel, 115

Meet the Author

J

EAN F. BLASHFIELD fell in love in Italy when she first visited the country as part of a college choir touring Europe. She couldn't stay long on that visit, but she has returned to Italy many times since then. The sounds, the beauty, the culture—they all draw her back time after time.

Blashfield was born in Madison, Wisconsin, and raised in Evanston, Illinois, a Chicago suburb. She graduated from the University of Michigan and then worked for publishers in Chicago and London. In Washington, D.C., she served as an education writer for NASA and the Federal Aviation Administration.

Early in her career, she developed the *Young People's Science Encyclopedia* for Children's Press. Since then, she has written more than 130 books, most of them nonfiction. She says that when writing a book for young people, she's often as challenged by what to leave out of the book as what to put in. This was especially true for this book on Italy because the country has such a rich and varied history.

Blashfield likes writing about interesting places best, but she also loves history, science, and almost every other topic. She has created an encyclopedia of aviation and space, has written popular books on murderers and house plants, and had a lot of fun creating a book on women's exploits called *Hellraisers, Heroines, and Holy Women*. She founded the *Dungeons & Dragons* book department at TSR Inc. and became avidly interested in medieval history.

She returned to Wisconsin when she married Wallace Black, a publisher, writer, and pilot. She has two children, Winston and Chandelle, both of whom are involved in university education. She is an avid Internet surfer, but she'll never give up her favorite pastime, going to the library.

Photo Credits